"A chilling analysis of how authoritarian politics promising protection are becoming hegemonic across the globe, from their most strident forms, to their creeping normalization in 'respectable' politics. Required reading for our pandemic times."
Luiza Bialasiewicz, University of Amsterdam

"A compelling analysis of the manifold threats currently facing pluralist democracies. As well as the excellent theoretical framing, the interviews allow the complex transformations of the sociopolitical landscape in Europe and beyond to be deconstructed. A must-read for graduate students and scholars alike."
Ruth Wodak, Lancaster University

LUKE COOPER

AUTHORITARIAN CONTAGION

The Global Threat to Democracy

BRISTOL
UNIVERSITY
PRESS

First published in Great Britain in 2021 by

Bristol University Press
University of Bristol
1–9 Old Park Hill
Bristol
BS2 8BB
UK
t: +44 (0)117 954 5940
e: bup-info@bristol.ac.uk

Details of international sales and distribution partners are available at
bristoluniversitypress.co.uk

British Library Cataloguing in Publication Data
A catalogue record for this book is available from the British Library

ISBN 978-1-5292-1779-7 paperback
ISBN 978-1-5292-1780-3 ePub
ISBN 978-1-5292-1781-0 ePdf

Cover design: blu inc, Bristol
Front cover image: @korpa / unsplash.com
Bristol University Press uses environmentally responsible print partners.
Printed and bound in Great Britain by CMP, Poole

For Natalie

Contents

Acknowledgements

Research for this book began with an eight-month fellowship (from September 2018 to April 2019) at the Institute of Human Sciences (IWM) in Vienna supported by the ERSTE Foundation Europe's Futures programme. Thanks to Ivan Vejvoda and all of the colleagues at the IWM for the hugely valuable discussions on these issues, which framed my thinking. Research for the book was also undertaken with the help of the LSE Visions of Europe project funded by the Open Society Foundation Initiative for Europe. Specific thanks to Titus Molkenbur and Ana Oppenheim for their assistance with research on the *Alternativ für Deutschland* and Law and Justice respectively, and to Zsuzsanna Szelényi for her advice and guidance on researching the Hungarian case. Thanks to Ruth Wodak, Mary Kaldor and the anonymous reviewers for feedback on the draft and proposal. Thanks also to Guy Aitchison for his collaboration on a related report on the new authoritarianism, and to Shalini Randeria and Nadine El-Enany for their very helpful comments at its LSE launch event.

ONE

On the March

Cleveland Grover Meredith Jr, or 'Cleve' to his friends, grew up in a wealthy suburb in Atlanta, Georgia in the 1970s and 1980s. He has two sons and a university degree. Meredith opened a car wash after graduating and is said to have a penchant for jet skis, motorcycles and big trucks (Bethea, 2021). On 7 January 2021, the day after the failed mob insurrection in Washington, DC, he was arrested by the FBI at a hotel in walking distance of the Capitol. They allegedly found him with a compact Tavor X95 assault rifle, a 9mm Glock 19 handgun and about 100 rounds of ammunition (Mustian et al, 2021). Friends had alerted the police after receiving a string of text messages from him in the previous 24 hours. 'I'm gonna run that Cunt Pelosi over while she chews on her gums … Dead Bitch Walking. I predict that within 12 days, many in our country will die' (in Mustian et al, 2021), they are alleged to have read. Meredith had missed out on the action the day before. His car broke down and he arrived late in Washington, perhaps a stroke of good fortune for the city's residents and politicians on an otherwise dark day in American history. But like many in the Trump movement his personal story has inevitably drawn the attention of those asking *why?* How had this mob insurrection been allowed to take place in the heart of America's democracy? And what ideas had settled in the minds of the rioting participants that led them to believe they were acting in the name of a noble cause?

A discussion of the range of authoritarian threats globally can hardly be limited to the United States. But perhaps inevitably we are repeatedly drawn to the figure of Donald Trump, the property tycoon cum reality TV show personality, who has now left the White House. His extreme political nationalism, racist rhetoric and almost 'unreal', satire-like personality spoke to the sense that we are living at a harrowing moment in global history. Breaking totally with the politics of multilateralism, Trump declared 'America first', railing against corrupt trade deals, foreign wars, Muslims and immigrants. As the consummate outsider he saw the Washington-based political establishment as part of an international conspiracy against the interests of everyday Americans that had left 'rusted out factories scattered like tombstones across the landscape of our nation' (Trump, 2017). This sense of civilizational crisis was key to Trump's brand of racialized political authoritarianism. He spoke of an unravelling world in which the last hope of the American people lay in his hands. For many others, of course, Trump was an expression of the civilizational crisis, not the cure to it. It was a sign that the slow drift towards authoritarianism and ethnic nationalism globally had suddenly become an almighty gallop.

I completed the first draft of this book a few days after the American election. It was already clear then that American democracy faced an extraordinarily difficult 'transition', the term given to the period when the election is over, but the winner has yet to assume the presidency. Trump had always maintained he would reject the result if he lost – a position he had also taken back in 2016. Without any evidence, and after dozens of failed lawsuits, Trump repeatedly claimed the election was stolen. It was a quite outrageous lie. Timothy Snyder (2021) distinguishes between small, medium and 'big' lies. Authoritarians – and, for that matter, all politicians – often spout falsities of the small and medium kind. These can be outrageously malicious, such as the racist 'birther' movement that repeatedly claimed President Barack Obama was born in Kenya, not the United States. But medium lies of this order do not require the construction of an entirely false, alternate reality. By contrast, Trump's claim that the American election had been fraudulently stolen was a 'big lie'. It transitioned him into an almost totalitarian posture. He, and only he, now had the power to determine what was true, and what was false. No evidence or justification was required. Like in George Orwell's *1984* the words lose their meaning with this shift. They are detached of their moorings in an objectively real and measurable universe. Freedom becomes slavery, the discourse a mere cypher for the despotic arbiters of truth. Inevitably, the lie also posited an insurrectionary moment, because how else could democracy be saved from theft and manipulation if not through mass protest and militant, even armed, direct action? Thomas Jefferson and his colleagues had, after all, said in the American Declaration of Independence that those facing 'a long train of abuses and usurpations', which risked the creation of an 'absolute Despotism', had a 'right' and 'duty … to throw off such Government and to provide new Guards for their future security' (Committee of Five, 1776). So, *if* the election had been stolen, the events would seem very different to us. But, of course, this was simply not the case. Trump put forward the most threatening and barbaric of falsehoods.

The aspect of the events of 6 January 2021 which remains most shocking is not the fact that thousands of Americans answered Trump's call and attempted to overthrow the democratic government. But, rather, that the insurrection was allowed to happen. A woefully unprepared security detail was easily overwhelmed. This suggested some element of collusion within the state, even at the basic level of restricting police resources. While the details of this may become clearer over time, the chain of circumstances on the day more than speaks for itself. 'Nobody could tell me that if it was a group of Black Lives Matter protesters yesterday, they wouldn't have been treated very differently than the thugs that stormed the Capitol' (Sheerin, 2021), as the then President-elect, Joe Biden, rightly observed. But whether it was meticulously planned, or simply the deployment of chaos, the events of 6 January 2021 were a fitting end to Trump's presidency. He was – and is – a master of politics as an exercise in 'shock and awe' spectacle. He seemed to almost feed off the very outrage he inspired among his critics.

This book analyses the rise of the authoritarian practices and symbols that Trump encapsulates as a form of hegemonic politics (Gramsci, 1971). Hegemony simply refers to the dominant ideas and political forces in society. When different parties jostle for leadership and influence in society, engaging in a 'battle of ideas', and seeking to move, in one way or another, away from the status quo, they are practising hegemonic politics – a process that can involve trying to adjust what citizens take for granted, that is, their 'common sense'. The *fact* of pluralism is central to a hegemonic analysis. Ideas are fluid and changing, individuals apprehend events in distinct ways, and a variety of values and outlooks will always co-exist within a society. So, the question political actors of all stripes universally have to engage with is, 'how do I convince people who do not agree with me on everything to support and vote for me anyway?' A related issue a hegemonic analysis raises is the fluidity of connections between leaders, elites and peoples. A hegemonic analysis is neither wholly 'top down' or 'bottom up'. It recognizes that outcomes, that is, what happens, will usually reflect the interaction between leaders, elites and peoples. This also has to take into account 'the outside world'. Ideas within society are formed not simply through its internal dimensions, but also by the interaction with other societies. This is particularly important for contemporary authoritarianism, which involves a hostile disposition towards 'foreigners'.

Trump was – and is – an astute practitioner of hegemonic politics, especially in his ability to pull behind his presidential campaign relatively more moderate, traditional strands in

American conservatism. He succeeded in holding together a broad electoral coalition despite his very hardline, far right leadership. Trump cultivated a frenzied group of fanatical supporters but was still able to reach well beyond this core even after his first term in office. Indeed, this returns us to the figure of Cleveland Grover Meredith Jr, who fantasized about assassinating the speaker of the House of Representatives. And may have realized his warped dream were it not for the actions of his friends and the FBI officers that acted on their tipoff. Trump believed having a loud group of angry, extra-parliamentary supporters was helpful in cultivating the rage and anxiety that he was able to feed off. He also took advantage of the fact of pluralism artfully. The polarization between progressives and conservatives in US politics was turned into a weapon. His message to moderate Republicans was simple: whatever they felt about him, the alternative, a Democratic Party that was supposedly in hock to the radical left and China, was worse. In other words, they had more in common with Trump than his dangerous, unpatriotic opponents.

This book is an investigation into this type of authoritarian politics and its global spread. It is a politics Trump typifies but is far from his exclusive preserve. The last decade has seen a coterie of 'strongmen' leaders emerge on the world stage. Narendra Modi in India, Viktor Orbán in Hungary, Jarosław Kaczyński in Poland, Rodrigo Duterte in the Philippines, Jair Bolsonaro in Brazil, are all examples of how democracy faces dangerous new threats. I also add to this list the sweeping centralization of power seen in China under Xi Jinping – a political change within a non-democratic system that has deepened its totalitarian features. The book plays particularly close attention to the contrast between Trump and Xi (see Chapter Five). Under their stewardship the United States and China arrived at a new low in their diplomatic relations. This standoff is revealing of the new authoritarianism, which is heavily laced with political nationalism. International politics is viewed in 'zero-sum' terms, that is, any gains for the nation are seen as necessarily coming at the expense of others. It sees legitimacy as derived by pursuing the interests of 'us', the insiders, the people, against 'them', the foreigners. Alliances and relationships are inevitably fragile in this context, as they are shorn of even the slightest pretence to a set of values and principles. They instead uphold a purely self-interested view of power.

I refer to this in the book as authoritarian protectionism. This is a mindset common to the new challenge to democracy that observes a simple maxim, 'the world will end for others, but not for us'. By putting it in this way, I hope to draw attention to the sense of existential threat and crisis that is animating the desire for *protection* among populations across the world. Whether they are material or imagined, these insecurities are 'real' in the simple but important sense they are formed through actual human conflicts, experiences and arguments. Many of us saw Trump's invocation of an 'American carnage' from which he was the only possible saviour as both absurd yet reflective of a real set of conditions: a nation that had allowed inequality and financialized deindustrialization to run out of control. Trump, in many respects, represented the globalized elite his rhetoric excoriated. But regardless of these inconsistencies his message found an audience and appeal among millions of his fellow citizens. In 2020, Trump added over 11 million votes to his 2016 haul – an extraordinary feat given the chaos of his administration and abysmal handing of the COVID-19 pandemic. Indeed, even before his supporters' attack on the Capitol, the election period had already been established as a historic one for American politics. The 67 per cent turnout was the highest since 1900 – and, so, in effect, the highest level of participation across the entire democratic era.[1] So, an election that will be remembered as one of the darkest chapters in American history also saw the greatest ever level of popular participation. This remarkable re-energization of the democratic political field reveals an important paradox on the state of politics in this century, one which has implications far beyond the shores of the United States.

The return of meaningful political strife, pitching a leftish social liberalism against the new authoritarianism, represents an important change from the consensus seen at the close of the Cold War. Indeed, it has long been argued that the collapse of the Soviet Union in 1991 created a post-ideological moment in world politics. As alternatives to free market liberalism waned government took on a more technocratic colouration. The very expansion of democracy had thus generated a post-democratic condition (Crouch, 2004). Left–right distinctions narrowed, leaving political competition gutted of the ideological moorings that gave it meaningful content and ignited emotive responses (Mair, 2013, p 253). As parties scrambled for the political centre, voters inevitably had less choice available as the policy options narrowed – hardly a great advertisement for democratic systems (Mouffe, 2005). It was always possible that this could leave parts of the electorate feeling disenfranchised. Since the 2008 financial crisis, authoritarian protectionism has filled this void. In democratic societies, a toxic mix of racism, spiralling economic inequality and insecurity and disillusionment with existing institutions, has encouraged anti-system voting (Hopkin, 2020). The extraordinary rise of China has also radically thrown into question a core assumption of the peaceful revolutions in 1989, which held democracy to be the only path to prosperity.

This new phase of politicization brings dangers and opportunities in equal measure. During the interwar period the new democratic political systems based on universal adult suffrage were wracked with conflict. Far from having a problem of technocratic agreement, they instead exhibited an extreme lack of consensus. As Eric Hobsbawm put it, this meant democracy became 'a mechanism for formalizing divisions between irreconcilable groups' rather than a means to establish a functional government (Hobsbawm, 1995, pp 140–141). The past does not repeat itself, at least not in a simplistic way. But it does provide certain warnings. One lesson which might be drawn from the interwar period and the 'consensus' era of the 1990s lies in how democracy has to contain and manage a fundamental contradiction (Mouffe, 2009): too much consensus and political debate loses its meaning; too much polarization and democracy risks breaking down. Democracy also depends on different groups trusting institutions and being 'good losers', that is, accepting political competition means that we cannot always win. If this trust no longer exists, then even the best designed institutions will still lack a sufficiently strong socio-cultural foundation.

Democracy versus authoritarianism: some preliminary remarks

There is no single model of democratic or authoritarian states. Both these terms are best seen as 'ideal types' that exist at different poles on a spectrum. In specific cases, past and present, these distinctions are often fuzzy, as many states combine democratic and authoritarian traits. Political scientists have long recognized this complexity and attempted to come up with a dizzying array of labels to capture different types of political system. These include a set of conceptual descriptions of states that are neither wholly democratic nor wholly authoritarian, such as the hybrid regime (Gilbert and Mohseni, 2011), electoral authoritarianism (Morse, 2012) and illiberal democracy (Zakaria, 1997; see also Plattner, 2019; Wodak, 2019). Among states that are seen as consummately undemocratic there can also be important differences in how their institutions work. China and Vietnam, for example, have long been acknowledged as highly institutionalized one-party states. The post-1991 Ethiopian regime was also not democratic but succeeded in creating an efficient, well organized state that achieved strong developmental outcomes (Berhe, 2020). In contrast, authoritarianism can also prosper where institutions are weak. President Omar al-Bashir's autocratic rule in Sudan was an example of a fragmented authoritarianism, in which, rather than achieving outcomes for society, a poorly functioning state becomes a means for different elite groups to extract resources from the populace (de Waal, 2015, chapter 5). And this type of authoritarianism is possibly more common than its efficient, institutionalized cousin.

As Aurelien Mondon and Aaron Winter (2020) remind us, democracies are also more than capable of doing 'bad things'. What they call reactionary democracy is the mobilization of the core principles of democratic functioning ('the rule of the people') for regressive – indeed, paradoxically, undemo- cratic – ends (Mondon and Winter, 2020). The de facto rejection of the *universal* element of *universal* human rights was, for example, an important feature of the response to the September 11 terrorist attacks in the West. In the United States, torture, kidnap (discussed through the euphemism of 'extraordinary rendition') and state assassination became normalized governing principles of foreign and security policy with Guantanamo Bay its most shameful result. Democracy as a means to hold the powerful to account was clearly diminished by the use of an overwhelming power capability in this way. It also illustrates the tensions in the relationship between the language and practice of democracy. For declaring oneself a part of the freedom-loving peoples can veil anti-democratic actions. Indeed, more than just a cynical use of language, this reflects part of the governing practice of many powerful states that are able to declare an exception from the rules that they insist others follow (Chatterjee, 1991).

Given this sea of complexity and variation the book does not offer a new typography of democratic and non-democratic regimes. Instead, it seeks to uncover common patterns that can be observed in spite of the wide institutional unevenness we find across different political systems. The book starts with a basic working conception of democracy and treats authori- tarianism as a relational category defined in opposition to it. Democracy is defined broadly as the co-existence of formalized systems of representation and substantive empowerment. The former refers to the rules-based procedures and institutions that regulate democratic practices. The latter denotes the conditions that make possible the meaningful ability of citizens to determine their own life choices and to have a say over political institutions that are responsive to their demands (Kaldor and Vejvoda, 2002, p 162). This normative conception, which depicts democracy as we would like it to be, not as it is necessarily practised in specific cases, opens up space to critique the status quo. What Mondon and Winter (2020) refer to as reactionary democracy, for example, could be seen as systems of governance defined by the presence of formal representation and institutions but the absence of substantive empowerment. The formal and substantive approach is also broad enough to allow for the possibility of future transformations, rather than treating existing norms as the end point of humanity's democratic experiment. This might include the extension of direct, economic or deliberative democracy, or the creation of global democratic spaces. In contrast, authoritarianism is defined by its attack upon both formal and substantive democracy. Authoritarians seeks to create, or *have created*, systems based on the monopolization of power by an oligarchic elite – usually combining political and economic interests. This simple relational definition means that where authoritarianism advances, democracy must decline – and vice versa. Furthermore, it follows that my definition of authoritarianism goes beyond 'reactionary democracy'; for it is defined by its attack, either openly or implicitly, on democratic life.

The march of authoritarianism is uneven but global in reach

The last three decades following the revolutions of 1989 have seen a sharp growth in international interconnectedness, global institutions and trade and financial ties that is often referred to as globalization (sometimes also dated to the restructuring of Western economies through financialization from the mid-1970s onwards). This period has seen a rise of non-Western powers on the world stage, but in an international system that remains decidedly plutocratic. Smaller states have a particular need for alliances to protect their interests in this globalized order – a process that achieves its highest formal expression in the European Union (EU), which supercharges the sovereignty of its smaller members. The G20 countries – comprised of 19 major national economies plus the EU – today dominate the international order, representing 90 per cent of global GDP, 75 per cent of world trade and two thirds of its population.

What happens in these core states will have an outsized impact on the ideological complexion of the wider world. And an uneven but clear trend over the last decade can be observed towards a new cycle of authoritarian politics. In India, Narendra Modi has pursued a hardline ethnic nationalist agenda, including ending autonomy for Kashmir, as well as introducing a discriminatory citizenship law that seeks to de facto disenfranchise non-Hindu minorities (Chacko, 2020, 2018; Rogenhofer and Panievsky, 2020). In China, Xi Jinping has aggressively centralized political power since he assumed office in 2012. He has abolished presidential term limits, written 'Xi Jinping Thought' into the Chinese constitution, and built a techno-surveillance state that has dramatically increased the presence of the party in the country's economy and society (Economy, 2018; Pei, 2020). In Brazil, Jair Bolsonaro is seeking out a new, quasi-militarized Bonapartism, packing his inner circle with military affiliated figures in a politicization of the armed forces not seen in the democratic, post-1985 era (Boadle, 2020; see also Hunter and Power, 2019). In Russia, Vladimir Putin presides over an autocratic state and shows little interest in giving up power over two decades into his rule (Taylor, 2011; Rutland, 2014; Snyder, 2018).

Meanwhile, in the West, democracy's travails are far from limited to the crises in the United States. Britain's decision to leave the EU was animated by raw political nationalism (Valluvan, 2019; Wellings, 2020). The evolution of the Brexit process since 2016 has combined this with authoritarian themes, including the illegal prorogation of parliament in the fall of 2019. Among the remaining members of the EU, two states, Poland and Hungary, have established openly illiberal, authoritarian regimes (Bozóki, 2011; Grzebalska and Pető, 2018; Krastev, 2018). But the trend to increased influence for the populist radical right touches most others (Muis and Immerzeel, 2017). Crucially, this includes the 'strategic interaction' (Szöcsik and Polyakova, 2019) between the centre right and the far right. Orbán's Fidesz party, for example, remains a member, albeit nominally 'suspended', of the European People's Party, the network of centre-right parties, and has cultivated a deep, but largely hidden, relationship with the German business and political elite (Szabolcs, 2020).

The premise that changes among the G20 states will be at least 'semi representative' of the world as a whole is also borne out by big data analyses of the state of democracy in the world's 195 countries. In 2018, the annual report of Washington-based think tank, Freedom House, had recorded its thirteenth consecutive year of global democratic decline, explicitly citing the troubling situation in the United States in this regard (Freedom House, 2019). Other studies are more circumspect about the *extent* of the backsliding from democracy occurring but they agree it is happening (Bermeo, 2016; Mechkova et al, 2017). They also note that the trend of elected leaders choosing an authoritarian path has become a more widespread threat to democracy compared to the traditional military *coup d'état* (Svolik, 2019).

This critical assessment of the current state of democracy internationally means that the 'genie is out of the bottle'. The forces of authoritarianism are now too strong to make this anything other than a long-term and polarized struggle between progressive democrats and authoritarian nationalists. Political scientists and historical sociologists sometimes discuss such 'long run' effects on society as *path dependence* (for example see Goldstone, 1998; Mahoney, 2000; Lawson, 2006), referring to how a particular chain of events in the past has a powerful influence on the present and future timeline. This recognizes that once ideas take hold in society and are backed up by institutions they can become 'sticky', that is, take on a persistence that makes them hard to overthrow. Establishing well organized parties and movements offers resources and capacity, while affinity for ideas within society provides these groups with political and cultural reach into the wider social fabric. Taken together this means that once authoritarian forces gain a foothold they are hard to dislodge. Financial resources can be raised from supporters and access to the mainstream media assured. Even when authoritarians are outside of government, they can assert a strong hold on political culture as an opposition bloc and threat to the status quo. Marine Le Pen's National Rally party in France, for example, have been kept out of institutional politics at the national level largely because of the specificities of the electoral system. But she and her supporters enjoy a huge platform with which to shape the terms of French political debate.

Authoritarian forces in office amplify these dangers, and the path dependent effects become potentially more long-lasting. In this situation, they can actively mould state and society around their interests. Putin, to take the most developed example of this trend, has gradually transitioned from an authoritarian-minded leader in a new democracy to making only the shallow pretence of holding a legitimate mandate. The Russian leader still enjoys public support and in the 2012 presidential 'election' he may have won a majority fairly in a hypothetical second round runoff. But he instead insisted on a fraudulent first round landslide (Snyder, 2018, chapter 2). When he admitted doing so (Snyder, 2018, chapter 2) he exhibited the 'shamelessness' of the contemporary authoritarian mindset (Wodak, 2019). By establishing his personality as synonymous with the Russian state itself Putin has therefore sought out a permanent authoritarian rulership. This almost goads the democratic opposition to think in revolutionary terms and moves the strategic horizon into the longer term.

The attempted murder of opposition leader, Alexei Navalny, and the mass protests that broke out following his arrest on return to Russia in January 2021, illustrate the great importance of this extra-parliamentary dimension of the democratic resistance. In the long period of conflict ahead, this may prove to be the reality that democrats face in many other states.

Authoritarians have established themselves in many states as a political presence and 'bloc' that forms part of the national debate. Now that this Rubicon has been crossed efforts to delegitimize these forces become harder. And makes the fight for the future of democracy a long-term one.

Authoritarian protectionism: the scope of the book

Democratic politics *in toto* is struggling to cope with a series of disruptive social forces facing the human condition. A part of the problem may be the lack of substantive democracy. If citizens do not believe that institutions are responsive to their demands, or that conditions in society provide them with the opportunities to lead productive lives, they may lose faith in the formal institutions of democracy. They may also be prone to 'beggar thy neighbour' thinking that argues they have partisan interests, for example as an ethnicity or nation, that are more important than formal democratic rules and justify overriding them (Svolik, 2019). Democracies also face the challenge that the outcomes citizens desire may be difficult to bring about without international cooperation. Democratic sovereignty in a particular state has to take account of the existence of other such democracies, each with leaders that have their own mandates and commitments, and potentially demand different goals. The EU has shown how difficult it can be to reconcile conflicting (democratic) demands in the arguments over the Eurozone (Nicolaidis et al, 2018). Even in times of stability the 'many-state' structure of international politics creates avenues for conflict between societies. But in times of crisis this is doubly the case. For the global order provides a host of 'others', that is, peoples, nations, ethnicities, etc, that can be blamed for systemic failings.

Developing these points, the book puts forward 'authoritarian protectionism' as a paradigm to understand the contemporary challenge to democratic politics. It has particularly negative implications for the basis of trust in a democracy. It seeks to persuade members of the insider group (usually the ethnically defined nation) that their partisan interest to survive and thrive in this violent world requires the defeat and suppression of 'others'. Because this need for national–ethnic supremacy overrides all other considerations, the rights and freedoms of outsiders are called into question. In addition, once members of the insider group are persuaded that their partisan interests are more important than democratic functioning, then they may be willing to sacrifice institutions to secure their position (Svolik, 2019).

The book elaborates further on these premises by arguing that authoritarian protectionists pursue a simple three-step logic to construct political legitimacy. First, homogenize the nation around a single predominant ethnic group, explicitly or implicitly; second, define this group's partisan interests as counterposed to their enemies, within or without; and, third, invoke a temporal emergency, a sense of existential risk which endangers the nation, perhaps drawing on semi-apocalyptic themes. The latter may also construct a victimhood fantasy: the belief, for example, that the ethnic majority are being trampled on by an arrogant, cosmopolitan elite, or overwhelmed by the immigration of cultural 'others'.

To develop this argument the book focuses on what Cas Mudde (2019) has called the 'fourth wave' of the post-war far right, which has unfolded across the first two decades of the 21st century. In this period, open and explicit fascism of the type found in the shameless neo-Nazism of the Greek Golden Dawn Party is still a fringe tendency. Instead, at least in liberal democratic societies, the fourth wave is predominantly defined by what Shalini Randeria (2019) refers to as 'soft authoritarianism', a drift towards despotic rulership, rather than a revolutionary break (see also Keane, 2020). The ideological and organizational convergence between the far right and the traditional centre right, involving the professionalization (and, to some degree, relative moderation) of the former in combination with the radicalization of the latter (see Renton, 2019) forms part of this transformation. This has implications for the broader delegitimization of democracy as a mode of government on the world stage. China's rise, and the sweeping despotism and ethnic nationalism seen under Xi Jinping, adds further momentum to this process which sees democracy being called into question. The country's industrial power radically challenges the notion that liberal democracy is *the* route to a prosperous future.

Taken together this means that the 21st century will be defined by a struggle between democratic internationalism and authoritarian protectionism in the throes of mounting social crisis.

This analysis is developed across four further chapters and a conclusion. Chapter Two ('Them and Us') introduces and develops the concept of authoritarian protectionism, drawing out points of similarity and difference between the various forms this politics has taken globally. Chapter Three ('"I Will Protect You"') situates the rise of authoritarian protectionism in a long crisis of the 21st century characterized by ecological breakdown, runaway inequality and broken geopolitical relationships between states. Chapter Four ('Pandemic Politics') analyses the relationship between authoritarianism and the global COVID-19 pandemic, identifying how there is no single authoritarian response to the global crisis. Chapter Five ('Sino-America') offers a comparative analysis of the highly distinct, in institutional terms, form of authoritarian protectionism in China and the United States. Finally, the concluding chapter returns to the questions drawn from Gramsci in Chapter Two and addresses them directly in light of the analysis developed across the book as a whole. It also puts forward what I call 'a radical politics of survival' as an alternative to the threat of authoritarian protectionism.

TWO

Them and Us

> Let them call you racist. Let them call you xenophobes. Let them call you nativist. Wear it as a badge of honour.
>
> *Steve Bannon, speaking at the 2018*
> *conference of National Rally*

Normalization. This term has dominated much discussion of the new authoritarianism and the threat it represents to democratic societies. And rightly so. For we can argue that normalization – along with its antithesis, marginalization – provides a critical criterion to assess the success of any insurgent political project: to what extent are its ideas and values diffusing across society and becoming embraced, such that they might even be considered a new 'common sense'? The Italian Marxist Antonio Gramsci is well known for his preoccupation with this question of how the matrix of cultural ideas intersected with economic conditions to allow for transitions between the dominant (or hegemonic) politics of a society. Often this would engage the methodologies socialists might use in order to win power and build an egalitarian society. His outlook challenged 'vanguardist' politics, emphasizing instead how a living basis for ideas had to form within society itself as a condition for successful state-level political efforts. But imprisoned by Benito Mussolini for 11 years before his premature death at the age of 46, Gramsci was equally concerned with how far right discourses could enter the body politic. This involved normalizing themselves as organic to the feelings and passions of certain social groups, in order to create the basis for a fascist takeover. A sense of this dual concern with the construction of progressive and reactionary hegemonies can be uncovered in his *Prison Notebooks* through reading his observations on how socialists might win support in parallel with his analysis of the rise of far right, nativist thought.

Gramsci argued that the process of 'mass creation' necessary for transforming the dominant ideas in society could not happen through the mere declaration of 'a personality or a group ... on the basis of its own fanatical philosophical or religious convictions' (Gramsci, 1971, p 341). Instead all political blocs aiming to achieve power in society had to find a foundation for their ideas among groups in society. 'Mass adhesion or non-adhesion to an ideology', he wrote, 'is the real critical test' (Gramsci, 1971, p 341). A party that builds up a core base of support could pursue a wider battle of ideas. All 'hegemony-seeking' groups need such a foundation. But they do not need a formal majority and may not retain any political commitment to a democratic society per se. Far right parties may only need a critical mass of adherents if they win support from key sections of the elite – a process that played out in the fascist takeover in Italy and Germany, which involved formalized (Italy) and episodic (Germany) coalitions.

Whether of the right or the left, successful blocs, Gramsci added, are defined by their symmetry to the 'demands' of history, that is, they adapt their strategy and messages to historical circumstance:

> Any arbitrary constructions are pretty rapidly eliminated by historical competition, even if sometimes, through a combination of immediately favourable circumstances, they manage to enjoy popularity of a kind; whereas constructions which respond to the demands of a

complex organic period of history always impose themselves and prevail in the end. (Gramsci, 1971, p 341)

For Gramsci social conditions inherited from the past provide a site of experimentation for ideological forces seeking
leadership in society. Groups that successfully melded their
ideas to existing trajectories of economic and cultural change
could be more confident of success. Normalization of their
ideas and values would lay the basis for transformative change.
Whereas those that were unable to grapple with these shifts
within the cultural and economic structure of society itself
would remain marginalized.

Gramsci's discussion of the Boulangists raises a number of
questions that can frame investigation into contemporary
authoritarianism. One of several European movements (see
Saull, 2014, pp 34–37) that emerged to prominence in the
economic turmoil following the financial panic of 1873, the
Boulangists advocated hardline, expansionary ethnic nationalism to revenge the French defeat in the Franco-Prussian
War of 1871. As with today's authoritarianism they used the
lexicon of national resistance to build a cross-class movement,
including sections of the working and middle class, as well part
of the traditional elite. Gramsci was critical of the economistic
way of thinking about such forces that starts with the question,
'who profits directly from the initiative under consideration?'
(Gramsci, 1971, p 166). By starting with this Marxism freed
itself, he argued, from the need for evidence-based analysis.
Instead a 'simplistic' and 'fallacious' form of reasoning was
established which stated the truism that a part of the elite would
profit, meaning no further explanation was needed (Gramsci,
1971, p 166). By assuming a set of economic objectives were
hidden from view and of primary importance to explaining
their rise, this approach occluded exploring how capitalism and
ideology intermixed. In contrast, his five alternative questions
sought to uncover the relationship of such movements to the
sociology of the times:

1. What is the social and class profile of those turning to the far right?
2. What impact has this new authoritarian bloc had on the rest of society as a whole? How has it changed the balance of forces?
3. What is the 'political and social significance' of the demands put forward by the movements' leaders which have found popular support? 'To what effective needs do they respond?'
4. How do the means the movement pursues relate to the supposed ends?
5. Is there a tension between the ends the followers expect and those that are likely? (Adapted from Gramsci, 1971, pp 166–167)

Gramsci argued that only once preliminary conclusions are reached in these five areas could we ascertain the class contradictions between the stated goals and substantive practices of far right movements. This seems highly pertinent to how we think about the 'moral' underpinnings of the new authoritarian right. Indeed, we can hold these questions in mind as we move through the analysis in this book, drawing out at each stage the dynamic interrelationship of capitalism to hegemonic politics.

As a starting point, consider the simple example of Trump's tax policy. His huge tax cuts of well over a trillion dollars reduced the US corporate rate to 21 per cent and created a situation where – for the first time in a hundred years – billionaires were paying a lower tax rate than every other income group of Americans (Saez and Zucman, 2019, chapter 1). But how far would we get in assessing the ideological bloc that Trump represents if we discussed his political movement in these terms alone? Could we really say that this constitutes the *true, hidden purpose* of Trumpism as a popular movement? For sure, the economic logic and interests at play reveal an important contradictory element of the Trump story. But on its own this tells us little about the nature and significance of his 2016 victory.

Part of the missing element lies in the moral claims and values involved in a bid for hegemonic leadership in society. These require the construction of a sense of community with a shared interest and set of goals. If individuals believe that the political bloc represents the interests of the community, they may look beyond any direct economic disadvantage or, at least, relativize and deprioritize it. Nations and nationalism have always been historically potent forces in this regard. They have an extraordinary capacity to inspire self-sacrifice; most of all in the willingness of individuals to risk their lives in the service of the nation (Anderson, 2006, pp 7–8). But nationalism does not usually require a sacrifice of this nature. Rather in most instances it simply convinces supporters that their interests are shared among the entire national community – and often sharply counterposed to those outside it.

To help us evaluate these discursive foundations of nationalism consider Nancy Fraser's distinction between redistribution and recognition (Fraser, 1995). As she explains any bid for hegemony, whether from the right or the left, will make moral claims that address these dimensions of political life:

Every hegemonic bloc embodies a set of assumptions about what is just and right and what is not. Since at least the mid-twentieth century in the United States and Europe, capitalist hegemony has been forged by combining two different aspects of right and justice—one focused on distribution, the other on recognition. The distributive aspect conveys a view about how society should allocate divisible goods, especially income. This aspect speaks to the economic structure of society and, however obliquely, to its class divisions. The recognition aspect expresses a sense of how society should apportion respect and esteem, the moral marks of membership and belonging. Focused on the status order of society, this aspect refers to its status hierarchies. (Fraser, 2019, np)

In this sense, redistribution and recognition can be seen as diverse spectrums that *all* political forces address, either explicitly or implicitly. Movements seeking gender equality, the rights of the LGBT+ community, an end to racial and ethnic discrimination, etc, each form classical examples of a 'fight for recognition'. By challenging unjust and oppressive status hierarchies they seek an expansion of democratic freedoms. When they are confronted with opposition – as they have been throughout history – their critics pursue a different politics of recognition, one based on a defence of existing status hierarchies that involves a set of alternative 'moral' claims about *whose* national community it is (Chatterjee, 1991). In this form, the politics of recognition is simultaneously one of exclusion: the assertion of identities based on masculinity, race and nation involves a refusal to recognize the legitimate place of other groups in the community and their substantively equal rights and freedoms.

As Trump's tax cuts demonstrate, *recognition* of these nativist impulses can be a powerful hegemonic device. If individuals within a higher status social group – say, White median income males – prioritize their own status-recognition, then they may be prepared to endure sacrifices at the level of distribution. Recognition in this form can also adjust how individuals think about distribution. Even if they are not benefiting materially citizens may believe that they are. In this way, a nativist politics of recognition extends the idea of solidarity and common cause 'upwards', that is, a group in the middle of society may believe their distributional interests are broadly aligned with those at the top. There is little factual argument to be made for this in the United States where the politics of distribution has for decades favoured the very wealthiest Americans over the middle classes, let alone blue-collar workers. But this perhaps simply underlines the potential potency of the 'moral' claim to hegemonic representation: who is the 'us' to be protected, and who are the 'them' from which the 'us' will be saved?

From authoritarian individualism to authoritarian protectionism?

Gramsci's work has long been drawn on to recognize the political and economic power of moral and cultural claims. The dramatic changes wrought by Thatcherism and Reaganism in the 1980s were recognized at the time as distinctive in the scale of hegemonic transformation they entailed. They shifted the reference points of political 'normality'. This Anglo-American revolution turned once marginal, hardline positions on market fundamentalism into a new norm that would globalize very rapidly.

Drawing on Gramsci, Stuart Hall (1988) argued that Thatcherism was a form of 'authoritarian populism', which successfully transformed accepted political norms, combining strongly conservative themes of family values, traditional morality, law and order and deference to authority with free market individualism. Neither a wholly elitist, nor wholly insurgent, hegemonic movement, the power of Thatcherism as an ideology lay in how the 'move to new forms of social authority and regulation "above" [was] rooted in popular fears and anxieties "below"' (Hall, 1988, p 84). Crucially, Hall argued that from its earliest inception the *moral claims* of Thatcherism were primary, not secondary, features of its ideological story. They were the decisive means it used to build a popular, democratic majority: 'The moral language and agenda of Thatcherism was never simply an ideological convenience. It was always the "leading edge" of its populism' (Hall, 1988, p 85).

Thatcher's 1987 Conservative Party Conference speech, which came after her third consecutive election victory had secured a lasting political legacy, is a clear example of these conceptual moorings. '[O]ur political opponents are now feverishly packaging their policies to look like ours', she boasted (Thatcher, 1987, np). The statement was broadly accurate and reflected the hegemonic shift occurring. The central themes of authoritarian populism were also strongly present. Freedom and liberty were defined firmly in terms of individual egoism and the economic retreat of the state. '[N]o Party now dares to say openly that it will take away from the people what we have given back to the people', she said (Thatcher, 1987, np). These were then conjoined to her chosen collective, that is, the interests of the British nation and the perceived cultural foundation stones of national sentiment. The 'philosophy of enterprise and opportunity' would, she argued, restore 'confidence and pride' (Thatcher, 1987, np) in the project of Great Britain. She taunted her opponents by quoting the Labour manifestos of the 1970s, arguing her policy agenda would realize an 'irreversible shift ... of power ... in favour of working people and their families' (Thatcher, 1987, np).

As Hall argued, this seemingly radical discourse strictly limited the conception of liberty and empowerment to a *freedom to buy* or what he called 'possessive individualism' (Hall, 1988, pp 142, 144). In other areas of social life Britons were expected to uphold strict moral codes that conformed with traditional society, family values and law and order. 'Civilised society doesn't just happen', Thatcher argued, '[i]t has to be sustained by standards widely accepted and upheld. And we must draw on the moral energy of society ... [and] the values of family life' (Thatcher, 1987, np). Railing against permissive culture, her government would go on to introduce Section 28 in 1988, the infamously discriminatory legislation that banned schools and public authorities from 'promoting' homosexuality.

Thatcher prosecuted this authoritarian vision through a democratic majoritarianism. '[I]n this process of restoration / revolution', observed Hall, the right know 'the winning card is the democratic populist one' (Hall, 1988, p 126). The manner in which 'creeping authoritarianism [was] masked by the rituals of formal representation' (Hall, 1988, p 126) has strong parallels to today's ascendency of anti-democratic politics.

Narratives of national service, discipline and fortitude are popular motifs of the contemporary authoritarian imagination. These often imply – as we will come onto later – coded and un-coded conceptions of heteronormativity and masculinity which draw from the same ideological well of Thatcher: a strong law and order state rooted in an embrace of the status hierarchies of traditional patriarchy. The extent of this is uneven across national polities, reflecting the tempo and rhythms of historical struggles for recognition by oppressed groups. Not all of the new authoritarians have adopted the hardline traditionalism of the Law and Justice Party in Poland, for example, whose favoured presidential candidate, Andrzej Duda, railed against 'gender ideology' in his successful 2020 campaign. Nonetheless, authoritarian protectionism shares with the 1980s Thatcherism that Hall analysed a preference for the rituals and vocabularies of national awakening as a pre-eminent discourse.

Yet to draw a line of simple continuity between the 1980s and 2010s would occlude a set of striking differences between the contemporary authoritarian turn and the original neo-liberal moment. To make sense of this requires a moment of reflection on the intruding period of 'high liberalism' in the international order. According to Jeremy Gilbert, a Cultural Studies professor and prominent figure in the British left, Hall felt his original analysis of authoritarian populism had understated the capacity of neoliberalism to become attached to the liberal values associated with Clinton, Blair and their global co-thinkers. There is a hint of this in Hall's eviscerating critique of New Labour from 1998 that saw him remark, '[t]his is not the populism of Mrs Thatcher's neo-liberal Right' (Hall, 1998, p 13). But he went on to argue that Blair's sublation of the left and right ultimately aligned with Thatcherism. Hall complained, in particular, of how his 'corporate' and 'managerialist' vernaculars involved a 'deeply manipulative' representation which held the unchecked brutalities of the free market to be 'empowering' for ordinary citizens (Hall, 1998, p 13). By utilizing inclusive language to pursue the same economic agenda Blair pioneered what Fraser has called 'pro-gressive neoliberalism' (Fraser, 2019): a socially liberal politics of recognition with a distributional approach largely dictated by Wall Street and the City of London.

So where in this mix stands what we have referred to as the contemporary politics of authoritarian protectionism? The answer lies in the diminished status of the liberal individual in the philosophy of contemporary conservativism. Blair and Clinton shared Thatcherism's commitment to the idea of the rational individual as a fundamental market actor. But Thatcher defined the nation's character through individual hard work, self-betterment and family values, declaring as deviants and enemies those that failed to meet this criterion of Britishness. In contrast, Blair drew on the shift to globalization to render this vocabulary softer, less openly nationalistic and more inclusive, at least in its presentation. But he shared Thatcher's belief in 'meritocracy'. Government would provide individuals with some level of opportunity, and material outcomes would then be based on their work effort and abilities. In short, from Thatcher to Clinton the politics of distribution were broadly similar. The state would not redistribute for the common good but instead resources would, supposedly, flow to individuals on merit.

In its ideological *presentation* (the substantive politics being a different and more context-specific question) authoritarian protectionism pursues a quite different politics of distribution. In most cases, the individual as an actor that gets what they 'deserve' is not the crucial rubric of the new politics. Instead authoritarian protectionism is animated by a collectivist agenda, but in a deeply nationalist form.

Today the party of Thatcher has largely shaken off its 'get on your bike' individualism. Instead the unorthodox Tory campaign of 2019 (Cooper and Cooper, 2020) declared its intention to 'level up' Britain. Given a central cause of this uneven economic development lay in the long-term effects of Thatcherite deindustrialization in the 1980s, this was a major change in Toryism. When the COVID-19 pandemic struck the country, prompting shutdowns and an economic downturn unprecedented in peacetime, Johnson even argued it was not like the crisis of 2008 as his government would 'put the people first', an implicit criticism of Gordon Brown's Labour administration (Johnson, 2020). This was an incoherent shift in policy, which was unable to say, for example, *why* some regions were poor and others wealthy. Yet, the national collective, and not the egotistical individual, was now at the apex of Conservatism's answer to the *distributional* question.

Beyond the shores of Britain other examples illustrate a similar pattern of ideological justifications in which *collective protection* of the ethnic community is a key theme of the new authoritarian right. In Poland, the Law and Justice's child benefit programme known as 500+ introduced a system analogous to the social security provisions of many Western European countries. Despite this, their Polish critics on the centre right, steeped in the distributional politics of progressive neoliberalism, criticized the policy in economic terms, at one stage describing it as 'a festival of [fiscal] irresponsibility' (in Cragg, 2019). But even where there is little or no policy substance to the *claim of protection* this collectivist discourse has been a key component to the ideological offensive of the new authoritarianism.

Trump presents himself as the champion of the interests of the American working class against the liberal elite. On the campaign trail in Pennsylvania he acclaimed, 'this is the place where generations of tough, strong ... workers mined the coal, worked the railroads, forged the steel that made American into the greatest and most powerful nation in the history of the world' (Trump, 2020a). Ironically, given his seething criticism of the Democrats' alleged attachment to radical left ideology, Trump expressed, in this masculinized, nationalist form, a version of what Marxists refer to as the labour theory of value: the concept that holds the source of wealth in society lies in the collective labour of the working classes.

While the idealized image of the White American male is a clear fit to Trump's ethnic nationalist politics, perhaps more surprising is his attempts to reach Black male voters through the language of protection. In one campaign video, watched at the time of writing by 6.4m people on YouTube alone, a Black male army veteran describes how he was "homeless, sleeping in … [a] car, didn't have any hope for a long time", until, that is, Trump took office (Trump, 2020b). "Life is good now, life is worth living", he says. The showcased policy in the short film, 'Opportunity Zones', is revealing in what it illustrates about the transformation of right-wing discourse. This government programme provides capitalists with tax breaks on investments they make in low income areas (though the definition of the latter has been critiqued). It largely amounts to a massive handout to the upmarket real estate sector. As the *New York Times* reported, even on the minimal criteria of creating jobs in construction the programme had limited results, as it often supported developments that were already in the pipeline. 'The federal government', they wrote, 'is subsidizing luxury developments — often within walking distance of economically distressed communities — that were in the works before Mr. Trump was even elected president' (Drucker and Lipton, 2019). Building luxury apartments and shops that poor people cannot afford to use as a development strategy is almost self-evidently problematic. This gentrification model has also been criticized for driving up rental and property prices with subsequent falls in poverty levels tending to be attributed to low income groups moving out of the area (Layser, 2019, p 766). But the language of Trumpism and its very 'direct' delivery has the capacity to brush aside these criticisms. It constructs an alternative reality for the public in which Trump is the protector, and saviour, of the working class. In this hyper-ideological model nationalism and disinformation serve to disguise the policy substance.

Julius Rogenhofer and Ayala Panievsky's (2020) comparative analysis of the regimes of Recep Tayyip Erdoğan in Turkey, Narendra Modi in India and Benjamin Netanyahu in Israel highlights points of continuity and difference in the rise of this language of national protection. In the Turkish case, which has some parallels to the approach of the Law and Justice Party in Poland we have discussed, traditional neoliberal policies, such as privatization and labour market deregulation, are combined with a clientelist, welfare-based approach that carefully directs resources to Erdoğan's support base. Islamic NGOs run government-funded welfare programmes, which serve to mitigate the effects of the neoliberalism pursued at the macroeconomic level (Rogenhofer and Panievsky, 2020, p 1397). In Israel, Netanyahu's pursuit of the settler vote in the West Bank involves similar clientelist dynamics, 'spanning housing subsidies, integration into public education and support for settlers' organizations with close ties to the Likud and Yamina parties' (Rogenhofer and Panievsky, 2020, p 1399). In both the Israeli and Turkish cases distributional politics is based on an exclusionary conception of the deserving to whom resources should flow, one defined according to Jewish and Muslim identity, respectively. A politics of distribution based on ethnicity serves to disguise how these are class-divided populations with very varied levels of economic status and opportunity. Authoritarian protectionism is careful not to draw attention to these inequalities.

Modi's approach in India shares this exclusionary, ethicized conception of 'the people'. Yet, in its distributional ideology, it is a partial exception in the broader landscape of contemporary authoritarianism. The Hindu nationalist BJP are much more classically Thatcherite in their individualistic, economic doctrine. They depict 'the people' as market-savvy, entrepreneurial, consumerist, middle class and digitally literate individuals, united by their Hindu faith, patriotism and commitment to the development of India (Chacko, 2018, pp 543–544; Rogenhofer and Panievsky, 2020, p 1398). But this economic individualism remains a subordinate element within a project defined above all by ethnonationalism. Modi's attempts to create a state in which citizenship is based on ethnicity (Gopal, 2020), as part of a majoritarianism that denies minority rights (Chatterji et al,

2019), still places the *protection* of *Hindutva* (their racialized term for Indian identity) at the centre of his authoritarian vision.

Them and us: democracy against liberty, or liberty against democracy?

The differences outlined in the foregoing can be seen as a shift from what we might call the *authoritarian individualism* of the 1980s to the *authoritarian protectionism* of contemporary radical right thought. Reframing Hall's analysis of authoritarian populism in this way allows us to recognize how populism has been a continuous thread across this transition, but also observe how it takes on a much greater intensity in the authoritarian protectionism of today. Populist language and ideology is mutable and adaptable to different contexts, but views society as 'ultimately separated into two homogenous and antagonistic camps, "the pure people" versus "the corrupt elite", and which argues that politics should be an expression of the *volonté générale* (general will) of the people' (Mudde and Kaltwasser, 2017, p 6). Importantly, populists can use these distinctions with great linguistic freedom to expand the category of 'elites' to include a broad range of individuals and groups that are deemed opposed to the 'pure people'. In the Brexit debate, this saw a remarkable articulation of diverse groups all viewed as an uncontradictory expression of the 'will of the people', stretching from multimillionaire hedge fund managers to large numbers of poor and working-class voters (for a short summary of the data on class and Brexit see Butcher, 2019). The geographical reference points of this vote, with big majorities for Leave in deprived working-class towns like Grimsby and Leigh, was seized on by Brexit supporters. They soon labelled poor but multi-ethnic and Remain-voting inner city areas as part of an 'out of touch', 'metropolitan' elite. Using the vernacular of 'the people' in this way to dismantle class-based bonds of solidarity between groups is not new. Indeed, it stands firmly within the Thatcherite tradition. As Hall argued, Thatcher presented 'Labour as part of the "big battalions" ranged against the "little man" (and his family) oppressed by an inefficient state bureaucracy' (Hall, 1988, p 142).

Authoritarian protectionism, however, has moved the pendulum considerably further in its strong trend to the ethnic homogenization of the pure people. And this *necessarily* has implications for democracy. Cas Mudde and Cristobal Kaltwasser argue that (2017, pp 7–8), in its deconstruction of the general will, pluralism constitutes a compelling alternative to populism, for it recognizes societies have a diverse composition with different groups that require and deserve political recognition and freedoms. Indeed, pluralism contains a logic that necessitates a democratic politics. For the recognition of minority rights, in reference to either a political or ethnic grouping, protects the long-term interests of the majority by establishing the conditions that allow society as a whole to 'change its mind'. Today's majority may be tomorrow's minority. So, democratic rules have to allow for the possibility of change.

It follows therefore that the total rejection of pluralism is likely to undermine democracy. In their discussion of how liberal political freedoms and democracy should interact, Alexis de Tocqueville (2010) and John Stuart Mill (1989) famously warned of the danger that a 'tyranny of the majority' might emerge which imperilled minority rights. While heavily influenced by de Tocqueville's enquiry into democracy in the United States, Mill was, however, more critical and, to some degree, less elitist. In his commentary on de Tocqueville's work, he made a series of pointed references to slavery and patriarchy. He warned that 'in America as elsewhere, one entire half of the human race is wholly excluded from the political equality', noted how White riots of the majority against Black people and abolitionists 'inspire … a terror which the most arbitrary monarch often fails to excite', and observed solemnly that in 'American democracy, the aristocracy of skin, and the aristocracy of sex, retain their privileges' (Mill, 1977, np; see also

Prochaska, 2012). So, this danger that male ethnic majorities could persecute minorities and women, deny them rights, and justify it according to a 'heroic' national cause, has long been recognized. For Mill this created contradictory tensions between democracy and freedom.

Whereas most scholars of democracy see the contradictions between liberalism and majoritarianism as conceptually resolvable in theory, Chantal Mouffe argues persuasively that this is not the case. Rather this tension forms a living 'paradox', one that must be continuously and 'precariously' renegotiated through experimentation and adaption to changing circumstances (Mouffe, 2009, p 93).

The limits of pluralism and the risk of tolerating anti-democratic politics provides a classical illustration of this problem: at what point does the embrace of plural politics allow authoritarian politics to cultivate itself within the polity? Here contemporary authoritarianism rears its head as in many states it represents a coercive force that emerges internally to democratic systems of government, not as an external aberration imposed through, for example, a military coup. In most instances, authoritarians deny seeking a tyranny of the majority. Indeed, this politics does not generally 'name itself' as such, that is, openly declare its rejection of the rights of minorities. But we should be particularly concerned when it does so. Viktor Orbán's pursuit of 'illiberal democracy' in Hungary is striking in this regard. For it pursues a political philosophy that attempts to 'resolve' the democratic paradox – the potential contradiction between liberalism and majority rule – by rejecting the former in the name of the latter.

Zoltán Kovács is the international spokesperson for the Hungarian government. He became a particularly prominent figure in the European media during the migration crisis. Indeed, according to his office, between 2015 and 2018 he undertook between 5,000 and 6,000 media interviews. This illustrates the extent to which the Orbán government has sought to intervene at the international level to challenge

Europe's 'liberal elite'. Kovács argues openly that his government rejects liberal rights: "The legitimacy of a government should be coming from the people. And that is the electorate, so it is the will of the Hungarian people, what matters. Democracy is democracy because and by [sic] the will of the people" (interview with Zoltán Kovács, spring 2019). Here Kovács was following closely the party's ideological line. For Orbán puts it in identical terms: 'There is a majority, and it must be respected, because that is the essence of democracy' (Orbán, 2019, np). While liberalism and democracy do not *necessitate* one another, as such, the merits of their interconnection are nonetheless clear. For liberalism provide the rules-based system on which democracy depends, establishing the basis for fair electoral competition. Kovács et al strongly disagree with this position. The Orbán government instead asserts a philosophy of vulgar majoritarianism:

> 'No we don't need liberalism because liberalism – again, I'm a historian – is a set of ideas which is one approach to democracy. We firmly believe that the individual alone is not the natural and most effective building block of a society. We believe the families and local communities are essential. And all together, at the end of the day, the interests of the interests of the community, the well-being of the national or local community and the family comes beyond and comes above individual interests.' (Interview with Zoltán Kovács, spring 2019)

In embracing the mantle of anti-liberalism, the Orbán government says openly what others deny yet still pursue in practice. For the legal order and its capacity to protect minorities has been a central issue in the global offensive against democracy. In India, while the government has not decisively moved against constitutionality, this shift is nonetheless posited by Modi's increasingly open rejection of the idea that Muslim Indians are equal citizens with fundamental human rights. This backdrop of public racism places pressure on judges; and the government has applied a carrot and stick approach to wield influence in the court system. In 2018, four Supreme Court judges took the unusual step to speak out against judicial interference (Varshney, 2019, p 73). By contrast, other judges have been accused of pro-BJP bias and many fear for the future of the rule of law (Ayyub, 2020). In Poland, the Law and Justice Party has sought to replace the majority of judges with government appointees, a move which has been described as an attempt to 'create a Soviet-style justice system, where the control of courts, prosecutors and judges lies with the executive and a single party' (Buras and Knaus, 2018, p ii). While this did prompt historic legal action by the EU (Buras, 2019), it has not pushed back the core of the reforms, which have included making 92 per cent of members (previously, 32 per cent) of the National Council of the Judiciary political appointees (Tatala et al, 2020). And the prospects remain bleak (Tatala et al, 2020).

In the United States, the country's political history means that similar trajectories are expressed in a quite different vernacular. The new radical right often herald the 'blessings of liberty'. In response to the demographic challenge posed by greater multiculturalism to the support base of US conservatism, Republicans have for a long time pursued 'voter suppression': a euphemistic-sounding term for a range of tactics that have the effect of reducing access to the vote for often marginalized groups. These include making it difficult for voters to register, unilaterally closing polling stations leading to long journeys and waiting times to cast a ballot, electoral roll purges that mean voters have to sign up afresh, and requiring IDs, which many poor people do not have, in order to vote (for a summary of these practices in the 2018 midterm elections see Root and Barclay, 2018). These practices to reduce opportunities for opponents to vote were conjoined in 2020 by Trump's earth-shattering attack on democratic norms, calling the entire process into question and denouncing mail-in ballots as attempts at electoral fraud.

A rules-based legal system needs to protect against these breaches. But in the United States the judiciary is historically highly politicized and divided on party lines. Trump appointed three ultra-conservative judges to the Supreme Court, forcing through the third on the eve of the presidential election (see Chapter Five). The combination of a social context in which it is difficult for hardline conservatives to win the popular vote (due to increased public support for multiculturalism and social liberalism) and the country's constitutional framework has meant US authoritarianism does not necessarily cast itself as majoritarian. Unlike Orbán and Modi it often adopts an ultra-conservative jurisprudence. But in a similar manner to Orbán this variant of authoritarianism also 'dares to speak its name'. Whereas Orbán rejects liberalism in the name of democracy, US ultra-conservatives reject democracy in the name of liberty. America *is not a democracy, but a republic* has thus become a commonplace claim.

Consider Utah Senator Mike Lee's intervention into the 2020 vice-presidential debate. A Tea Party insurgent who joined Congress in 2010, Lee is widely seen as one of America's most right-wing, ultra-conservative populists. 'Democracy isn't the objective; liberty, peace, and prospefity [*sic*] are', he tweeted, misspelling prosperity, 'We want the human condition to flourish. Rank democracy can thwart that' (in Bryant, 2020). Lee was merely repeating a widespread view in Republican circles. John Yoo, a professor of law at Berkeley who infamously provided the Bush junior administration with a 'legal' justification for the use of torture, criticized the US left's discussion of constitutional reform in the *Financial Times*. 'All these changes supported by the left are supposed to make America more democratic', he said, but 'they overlook America was designed to be a republic, not a democracy' (Luce, 2020). Trump is often seen as an evil figure far beyond normal American conservatism. But the practice of voter suppression and the rejection of the ideal of America as a democracy is a common position of American conservatives. The Heritage Foundation, a think tank founded during the Reagan ascendency, provided the bulk of staffers to the Trump administration (Mahler, 2018). It illustrates the overlap between Reaganite Republicanism and the new radical right. In June 2020, the foundation published an essay, *America Is a Republic, Not a Democracy*, which stated, 'contemporary efforts to weaken our republican customs and institutions in the name of greater equality … run against the efforts by America's Founders to defend our country from the potential excesses of democratic majorities' (Dobski, 2020, np). It went on to make a series of breathtaking attacks on democratic politics. As arguably the most influential Washington-based conservative think tank it provides an insight into the kind of thinking we can expect to be promoted by the new, much more conservative Supreme Court (see Chapter Five).

In this sense, once political content is given to the pro- and anti-liberal postures of the American and Hungarian radical right, we can reveal their ultimate coherence. Both are grounded in a conservative religiosity combined with support for strong anti-egalitarian protections for property and capital. Orbán admits his anti-liberalism and the new American right confess their opposition to democracy.

In truth, neither of these doctrines are democratic and nor are they interested in the protection of genuine political freedom. Their openly expressed authoritarianism bodes ill for the world's future.

The hegemony of 'them and us': the ideological logics of authoritarian protectionism

Rather than being exceptional, recent events in America give an insight into a broader pattern we see unravelling globally. The American context provides a particularly striking illustration of what can happen when a part of the political and economic elite, primarily individuals and groups with a background in the Reaganite turn of US Republicanism, has decided that its interests can no longer be served through democratic systems of rule (on this see Mason, 2019, chapters 6–7). It represents a shift from a conservative, democratic individualism to an authoritarian protectionism that is increasingly anti-democratic and aggressively prioritizes the ethnic-national collective against a range of 'others'. Some elements of this at least are worryingly similar to Hannah Arendt's famous description of Nazism's rise to power as involving 'a temporary alliance of the elite and the mob' (Arendt, 1973). Even before the attempted insurrection on the Capitol by a far right mob, Trump had made little attempt to conceal his patronage of these forces. 'Proud Boys, stand back and stand by', he said, in response to pressure to renounce the White supremacist movement during the presidential debate at the end of September (Trump, 2020c). 'Standing by, sir', the group tweeted in response (Mahers, 2020).

Authoritarian protectionism provides a means to glue the elite and mob together. This involves a three-step logic that we introduced in the last chapter: establish an ethnically homogeneous people; aggressively support their partisan interests against 'others', within and outside the community; and warn of a 'temporal emergency', a civilizational struggle requiring decisive action to protect the nation.

The aforementioned essay, *America Is a Republic, Not a Democracy*, can be read as an exercise in the three step logic. Its chosen 'other', its enemy within, lies in what they call the 'democratic habits' of the American people, and the dangerous rise of progressivism, social liberalism, and the desire for socio-economic equality and racial justice. They hold this shift among the American majority to have made catastrophic breaches in the status hierarchies of family, nation and religion. This has allegedly abolished 'any meaningful differences between the sexes; denied the special place reserved under the law for the traditional family; replaced procreation with the equalizing power of "choice" as the basis of marriage ... treated good and bad students as equals ... [and] dissolved the difference between citizen and foreigner' (Dobski, 2020, np). We are told mournfully that this offensive against tradition has left 'religion, especially its Judeo-Christian form' on the 'sidelines of American life' (Dobski, 2020, np).

In this appeal to the desperate plight of Christianity, a middle America facing a series of existential threats to its way of life but dreaming of, indeed anticipating, a coming salvation, we find each element of the logic of authoritarian protectionism. America is defined above all as a Judeo-Christian space. The coded racialization present in this description of the national community is made explicit in the complaint that the 'difference' between citizen and foreigner has been 'dissolved'. Thus logic one – ethnic homogenization – is established and the alternative posited: an America where *difference* with the foreigner is cultivated again through the assertion of White national identity. A series of partisan interests (logic two) are, in turn, posited: the re-assertion of the traditional family, its gender roles and the Christian religion at the centre of American life, and the protection of the nation's White citizenry from the intrusions of 'foreign' multiculturalism. The jaw-dropping statement – which could have been lifted directly from the hyper-patriarchal dystopia in the novel and television series *The Handmaid's Tale* – that the basis for marriage is procreation and not a choice of co-habitation made by two individuals with equal rights, is a particularly shocking illustration of this extreme conservatism.

Meanwhile, the essay's core argument – that democracy is neither a historically necessary nor desirable element of the American constitutional system –mobilizes these partisan interests towards authoritarianism. The third logic, the sense of emergency, is curiously formed by the *mere demand* of Americans for greater democracy. This, we are told, must be resisted at all costs: 'If unchecked, these passions, so strongly animating a democratic people, can destroy the republican institutions that are its remaining hopes to maintain its political liberty' (Dobski, 2020, np). This cartoon-like villainy is difficult to take seriously until one remembers it emanates from a group that was at the centre of Trump's White House.

These millenarian fantasies, we should acknowledge, form out of real world events. Such anxious cries for help are a kind of psychotic reaction to social change. After all, it is true that America is becoming more multi-ethnic, not less. Furthermore, the demand for greater progressivism – from socioeconomic equality through to democracy, resistance to racism, and advocacy for the rights of minorities – is stronger in the United States today than at any period since the 1970s. A wellspring of White conservative anxiety and victimhood appears to have erupted in the face of these transformations.

Authoritarian protectionism in Hungary and Poland: the politics of blood and soil nationalism

In each wave of real social explosion through the crises of this century, these anxieties can be mobilized readily around authoritarian protectionist assumptions. By describing this sentiment as 'the world will end for others but not for us', we can draw attention to the role played by the transformed sociological context: the systemic disruptions and crises of the contemporary capitalist world (see Chapter Three).

In Europe, the so-called refugee 'crisis' has provided an early example of how the social explosions that will become more common across this century can be instrumentalized by authoritarians and made worse by traditional elites conceding to their demands. In most European iterations of authoritarian protectionism, the national people are depicted as 'under siege', their values and culture potentially overwhelmed, with the march of the 'invader': the non-White peoples seeking refuge on the shores of the continent. At the policy level what should have been a simple matter of providing legal routes for those exercising their international right to seek protection from war and violence, became a never-ending spectacle and catastrophe due to the repeated, failed attempts to 'stop the boats'. As securing the walls of fortress Europe fails, and migrants continue to arrive by unsafe, informal means, the spectacle of the crisis is beamed across the continent by the media, providing talking points for the new authoritarians that fit easily with their ongoing ideological campaign. No other event and policy failure over the last decade has provided more ideological impetus to the European radical right.

In Poland and Hungary, authoritarian protectionism casts the nation as a victim of out of touch EU elites determined to open the door to migrants in a bid to destroy the Christian identity of Europe. In a September 2017 interview, Beata Szydło, who served as Law and Justice Prime Minister between 2015 and 2017, argued they were merely concerned with the security of citizens. 'People in Poland, in public places, feel safe or at least much safer than in Western Europe', she claimed, before condemning the EU elite for 'an intentional project of destroying what so far has built our continent: safety, community, respect, wellbeing and our Christian roots' (Newsweek Poland, 2017). Orbán explicitly draws out the ideological conclusion of this in his rejection of liberal political freedoms, counterposing these to the stabilities and cohesion of nationality and religion. 'According to the liberal notion of freedom', he argues, 'you can only be free if you discard everything that involves you in belonging somewhere: borders, the past, language, religion, culture and tradition' (Orbán, 2019). His closing speech in the 2018 general election campaign made a series of civilizational, millenarian statements, presenting a vote for his party as part of a struggle to save Hungary from Muslim invaders:

Look around: the world we live in is not exactly peaceful. Europe is afflicted by a number of conflicts: armies are fighting immediately to the east of us; and there is the threat of a trade war between the European Union and the United States. But the greatest threat of all is posed by the millions of immigrants coming from the South, and Europe's leaders – in partnership with a billionaire speculator – have no intention of defending the borders, but want to let in the immigrants. This is the truth of the matter … Everyone who wants to preserve Hungary as a Hungarian country must go out and vote, and must cast both their votes for Fidesz. (Orbán, 2018)

In anti-Semitic terms, he argued that by supporting Fidesz voters would be rejecting the 'future that is intended for us in Brussels, in the United Nations and in the alchemical workshop of George Soros' (Orbán, 2018). In the 2020 Polish presidential election, which was won narrowly by the Law and Justice associated incumbent, Andrzej Duda, the alleged threat from LGBT+ and 'gender ideology' movements also featured prominently. In one campaign speech, Duda described LGBT+ rights as an ideology that was worse than Stalinism. His parents' generation, he said, did not overthrow communism 'so that a new ideology would appear that is even more destructive' (in *BBC News*, 2020a). This allows the threats allegedly pitted against the inner sanctity of the Polish nation to be cast as wide-ranging: feminist, gay rights and sexual liberation movements supposedly put the traditional institutions of family and marriage at risk; non-White, Muslim immigration seeks to destroy the ethnic and cultural homogeneity of the nation; and liberal political elites side with these groups against the interests of the common Pole.

Through these coded racial references logic one of authoritarian protectionism (ethnic homogenization) is established: the Hungarian and Polish nations are defined as ethnically pure people united by Christian faith, family and tradition. The nation stands together opposed to the foreign other.

Once this ideational foundation is in place logic two is established: only the party – of Fidesz and Law and Justice – can protect the partisan interests of the people from those forces wishing to destroy them. Crucially, each of the nation's foreign and domestic enemies are associated with the domestic political opponents of these parties. Law and Justice often refer to their rivals as the 'total opposition', defined against everything that the party and Poland stand for. Erosion of the democratic rules of the game, the underpinning of a competitive party system, becomes a natural step once the very existence of opposition is delegitimized. Law and Justice also share the vulgar majoritarianism of Fidesz. 'In a democracy, the sovereign is the people, their representative parliament and, in the Polish case, the elected president', argued Kaczyński in 2016, 'if we are to have a democratic state of law, no state authority, including the Constitutional Tribunal, can disregard legislation' (cited in Davies, 2018, p 2).

Law and Justice have also carefully cultivated a conspiracy theory around the Smolensk plane disaster of April 2010, which killed 96 people, including Law and Justice co-leader, Lech Kaczyński. Within the cultural ecosystem of the Polish far right it was repeatedly claimed the Law and Justice leader had been a victim of a Russian state assassination. Like Trump's refusal to disavowal the QAnon conspiracy, the party did not back it explicitly but simply allowed it to circulate, and implied the liberal government was responsible. Once it took off the implication was clear: Law and Justice's opponents were no longer 'normal' political competitors. Instead – by covering up the actions of a foreign power against the Polish people – they were guilty of an act of treason towards Polish society (Wilczek, 2010).

The aim of these moves is a form of total sovereignty. According to this logic only the political instrument of the party and its leaders can uphold the partisan interests of the White Christian nation. This closing down of the democratic space can also involve deeply solipsistic reasoning. Against the backdrop of his government's efforts to intimidate Hungarian civil society, creating a blacklist of 'foreign supported organisations' (*BBC News*, 2020b), Kovács argues that the very concept of NGOs is undemocratic because these organizations have "never been elected … never tested themselves at democratic elections" (interview with Zoltán Kovács, spring 2019). The free association and public criticism on which democracy depends is called into question by this hardline, authoritarian discourse.

Orbán's speeches (for example, as we have discussed, "[l]ook around: the world we live in is not exactly peaceful") also seek to convey this deep historicity, expressing the sense of temporal emergency (logic three). A world beset with fundamental, indeed 'civilisational' crisis serves to justify his authoritarian leadership. Law and Justice similarly conjure the image of a global system in deep crisis that only the party offers Poles protection from. Indeed, one supporter captured this disposition perfectly in an online post during the pandemic. 'There are various threats' of a 'civilisational' character, she wrote, 'the war in Syria and the one in Ukraine, gender ideology, danger stemming from the stupidity of the opposition. With such a background, coronavirus is *only one of many threats*' (in Never Again, 2020, p 2, emphasis added). We find similar remarks from Orbán in how he depicts the great stage of history with 'armies … fighting immediately to the east of us' while Europe and America face a new trade war.

Against this crisis-plagued context the task of Poles and Hungarians, these parties and leaders suggest, is not to rally to a universal interest, based on our common humanity, but a particularist, national one. As war raged overseas, and migrants fled to escape, these authoritarians would 'put the people first'. They would protect Poles and Hungarians against this inferno of despair and suffering.

The fate of other peoples is, at best, secondary for this nationalist form of authoritarian philosophy. Indeed, it seems to state quite unashamedly, 'the world may end for others, but not for us'.

'We the people': incentives and practices of the new authoritarianism in Europe

The depressed small town geographies of the post-industrial era in the West has cultivated a way of thinking about place and nation, which has often heeded the populist call for nationalist awakening and salvation (Rodríguez-Pose, 2018; Dijkstra et al, 2020; Rosenberg and Boyle, 2019). In these fragmented conditions, in which the comforts of national tradition and cohesion seem preferable to the realities of the present, the authoritarian protectionists have found a wide audience for the new politics.

Germany, for so long a stable voice of a centrist and liberal Europe, has experienced these effects with the rise of the *Alternativ für Deutschland* (AfD) (Cooper and Molkenbur, 2019). Compared to previous new parties on the German political scene its ascent has been rapid. The AfD has outperformed the 'left newcomers' of the 1980s (Greens) and the 1990s/2000s (PDS/Die Linke) in the rapidity of its rise in German politics. In the 2017 national elections it won 12.6 per cent of the vote and 91 seats in the Bundestag, making it the third largest party – although its support has waned since. Since its formation the AfD has undergone a continuous process of radicalization. It started life as a right-wing Eurosceptic party opposed to the Eurozone bailouts and morphed over time into a much more hardline, ethnonationalist party. Socioeconomic decline in the states of the former East Germany has been an important factor in the rise of the AfD. On average, the party won twice the vote share in the East it did in the West – though, in absolute terms, two thirds of its vote was drawn from the more populous Western states (Decker, 2018). While anti-immigration sentiment is hugely important to its electoral support, the outward migration from East to West has arguably been a much more significant factor in shaping the economic geographies that the AfD has found a receptive audience in. According to data compiled by *Zeit Online* between

1991 and 2017 some 3.68 million people moved from East to West – vastly exceeding the flow of people in the other direction (2.45 million) (Bangel et al, 2019). More than a quarter of those aged 18 to 30 left seeking new opportunities in the West. In tandem with a falling birth rate in the 1990s, this was a recipe for an ageing population and economic stagnation (Bangel et al, 2019). Areas that saw the largest falls in populations were those most likely to vote for the AfD in the 2017 election (Bangel et al, 2019).

The AfD follow the logics of authoritarian protectionism very closely and break many of the social taboos of post-Nazi Germany in the process. Björn Höcke is a leader of the influential *Der Flügel* ('the wing') hard-right faction of the party, which has been formally classified as an extremist organization by the German state (and consequently asked to dissolve by the party leadership). Referring to the Holocaust Memorial in Berlin, Hocke has lamented how, 'We Germans ... are the only people in the world who have planted a monument to shame in the heart of their capital' (in Kamann, 2017). Former leader, Alexander Gauland, has similarly engaged in the trivialization of Nazi atrocities. In a comment that amounted to a form of Holocaust denial he argued, 'Hitler and the National Socialists are just bird shit in 1,000 years of successful German history', appearing to dismiss the appalling atrocities carried out during the war as an unfortunate inconvenience (in Associated Press, 2018). Logic one of authoritarian protectionism, the definition of the nation in ethnic and racialized terms, sits easily with this attack on political correctness and the realities of German history. The AfD has often implied support for the so-called 'ethnopluralist' agenda, a euphemism used by the European far right to racialize national identities. This doctrine holds nations to be culturally and racially immutable. So, there is no place in this conception for non-White, 'alien' members of the community. Hocke has called openly for the expulsion of Muslims from Germany and Europe, telling supporters that once the party takes power, 'we will enforce what is necessary so that we can live our free life', and this means that the 'Bosporus … [will be] the border for the three great M's, Mohammed, Muezzin and Minaret' (in *Die Welt*, 2018). During the 2017 election campaign, then party co-leader Gauland also made an outrageously racist attack on the SPD's Deputy Chairman, Aydan Özoguz, who was born in Hamburg and has been a German citizen for more than three decades. Gauland argued regardless that he looked forward to the day 'we will be able to dispose of her in Anatolia' (in Bender 2017). In terms similar to the Polish and Hungarian radical right, Gauland and his colleagues repeatedly depict immigration as a mortal threat to the nation's sanctity: 'They want to take this Germany away from us … dear friends, it is almost something – in the past it would have been called an invasion – like a creeping land grab' (in Bender 2017). As the attack on Özoguz shows, targeted here are not only migrants, but the non-White. Germany is defined entirely as an ethno-state. The preserve of *true Germans* and *true Germans* alone.

These blistering racist provocations and ethnonationalist definition of Germany (logic one) connect readily with logics two and three of authoritarian protection. Germany and Europe are depicted in an emergency situation, a civilizational crisis formed through the non-White 'invasion' (logic three). And the party appeals aggressively to the partisan interests of its supporters to rise up and overthrow the liberal elite. The figure of Angela Merkel has formed a totem for their opposition, which often has a strongly misogynistic tenor. They call on Germans to resist not only Merkel and the Christian Democratic Union (CDU) but the 'Merkel-system' (in Bender, 2018), a sweeping reference to an allegedly out of touch cosmopolitan establishment. The AfD has even cynically taken up the slogan of the 1989 protests in East Germany, 'we the people', to promote its far right insurgency against multiculturalism and liberalism. Gauland has spoken, for example, of the need for a 'peaceful revolution' to overthrow Merkel's system (in Bender, 2018).

The initial emergence of the AfD shocked Europe largely due to how it appeared to challenge the assumption that contemporary German society had deep cultural reserves hostile to the resuscitation of ethnonationalism. Yet, in some respects, the events of the last five years demonstrate the truth of this observation. AfD supporters remain a small minority. And unlike in many other cases – notably, Poland and Hungary – where Muslim immigration has been near non-existent, Germany has provided refugee protection to very large numbers of people. In 2019, according to the UNHCR, Germany was home to 1.5 million refugees – the third largest number of any other state in the world (UNHCR, 2019). Yet, despite this, the AfD has stagnated. So, progressive leadership, at least relatively speaking, on the migration question, coupled with a public sphere in which hostility to the far right remains high, does appear to have made Germany more resistant to the toxic demands of authoritarian protectionism.

THREE

'I Will Protect You'

The first half of the twenty-first century will, I believe, be
far more difficult, more unsettling, and yet more open than
anything we have known in the twentieth century.

Immanuel Wallerstein, The End of the World
as We Know It: Social Science for the
Twenty-First Century *(2001)*

Historical sociologists have used the terminology of a 'long
crisis' to analyse past phases of human history marked by tur-
bulence and disruption. These phases of greater instability
saw an increase in warfare between states, popular rebellion
and revolution. Their underlying cause, insofar as a single one
could be identified, often lay in contingent processes taking
place in the ecological biosphere, regionally or globally. These
placed acute pressures on the development needs of societies.
Changing weather patterns leading to prolonged droughts, for
example, had particularly severe effects in low productivity,
predominantly agricultural societies. The spread of pathogen
diseases, especially when new points of connectivity between
societies have been established through war, trade or empire,
could also expose populations with little or no immunity to
illness, leading to terrible hardship and death.

The regional system of Europe, North Africa and Western Asia was hit brutally hard by the 'Black Death' in the 14th century – with the 'first wave' alone, running from around 1347 to 1352, killing around 50 per cent of the population of Western Europe (Belich, 2016, p 95). A disaster on this scale inevitably had a profound effect on the dynamics of these societies, driving rebellion, forcing structural changes, and conjuring 'prophecies and apocalyptic visions announcing the end of the world' (Federici, 2004, pp 31–32). In the 17th century, changing weather patterns created a similar but more global dynamic, as persistent and widespread drought brought war and revolution – extending from the Thirty Years War in Europe to the world's most prosperous polity, China, as the Ming dynasty fell (Goldstone, 1988; Parker, 2008). The complexity of the human relationship to our environment has shaped the terms of these long phases of crisis. 'Human relationships to the natural environment and short-term climate change have always been', as Brian Fagan argues, 'in a complex state of flux. To ignore them is to neglect one of the dynamic backdrops of human experience' (Fagan, 2001, np).

Are we witnessing a similar long crisis unfolding today? In a thoughtful set of remarks on the future sociology of our world, published at the close of the 20th century, Immanuel Wallerstein reminds us of a simple but pertinent point: 'historical systems, like all systems, have finite lives. They have beginnings, a long development, and finally as they move far from equilibrium and reach points of bifurcation, a demise' (Wallerstein, 1999, p 1). Against the consensus of the 1990s, he maintained the triumph of liberal capitalism after the Cold War was an illusion and that the first 50 years of the 21st century would be defined by a traumatic crisis of the system. These changes would represent a pivotal moment in the history of capitalism, a 'bifurcation', foreshadowing a transition towards a different historical system. Change was, in other words, inevitable but the nature and form it took was open: a matter of conflict, a battle of ideas, in the throes of the systemic turmoil and crisis.

These predictions seem prescient just over two decades later. The global challenge to democracy seen in this new period does appear to paradoxically have its roots in the fall of the Soviet Union, December 1991. The very moment of triumph for the liberal democratic model has had important downstream effects for world politics in this century with the key environmental, social and diplomatic challenges we face today reflecting the new global settlement established in the 1990s. Other crises in world history have been defined and analysed according to three metrics: environmental conditions and their impact on the human world; the productive capacities of the socioeconomic system; and the geopolitical relationships between societies (including their propensity for war). And we can similarly use this register to analyse the crises of the current century. We face historic environmental challenges in our relationship to the natural world; an economic system that has produced extraordinary levels of inequality; and a new multipolar world with no overarching, dominant power. The current crisis therefore shares some qualities with these earlier periods of disruption in history. Its distinctiveness lies, however, in how it is uniquely shaped by the ecological consequences of industrial capitalism. Unlike earlier crises experienced by international systems, in its 21st-century form the long crisis is distinctively *global* and *human* – it lacks the 'ecological contingency' of its forebears.

The imprint of industrialization on planet Earth is altering the biosphere and giving rise to potentially cataclysmic 'feedback loops' for human societies. But thanks to modern science we also have the incalculable benefit of forewarning. Sophisticated predictive models have been developed outlining the likely ecological effects if current trends are allowed to continue. Three decades ago, the Intergovernmental Panel on Climate Change (IPCC), a scientific advisory body created under the auspices of the United Nations in 1988, produced its first assessment report. As the *Financial Times* commented at the time, the message was stark: '[t]he world may warm up catastrophically unless swift action is taken to reduce concentrations of "greenhouse" gases' (Hunt, 1990). But to this day the international community has still not turned the tide on rising emissions. On the thirtieth anniversary of its first report the IPCC noted that 'global greenhouse gas emissions have continued to increase, leading to further global warming' (IPCC, 2020). In the period from 1990 to 2013 global CO_2 emissions rose by some 60 per cent (Khokhar, 2017), despite numerous agreements recognizing the need to act.

Current policies mean the world is on course for a 3-degree increase in temperature on the pre-industrial average by 2100 (ClimateTracker.org, 2020). This would mean the loss of entire ecosystems, desertification of arable land, a greater intensity of extreme weather events, and the melting of glaciers and the polar ice caps, leading to a rise in sea levels. Global temperatures are currently around 1 degree higher than the pre-industrial average with the effects on the biosphere already observable. There has been a long-term downward trend in crop yields, greater population exposure to wildfires and – significantly in the COVID-19 era – evidence that changing climactic patterns make it easier for diseases to spread through the global system (Watts et al, 2019).

To tackle this civilization-level threat two spheres of human activity have to work in tandem together: economics and geopolitics. At the geopolitical level states need to agree cooperative policies to re-orientate societies towards the goal of sustainable development. As not all states stand to be equally affected by climate change, this requires a recognition that 'global goods' should be pursued for the benefit of humanity as a whole. At the economic level systems need to be built for a just transition. This should seek public support for trans-formative changes in the level of demand for energy, and the source of supply, by ensuring those most able to pay, that is, the wealthiest states and classes, carry the burden.

Simple as this sounds, history demonstrates how difficult it is to get the geopolitics and economics to align in the right way. Consider the circumstances that existed in 1990 when scientists called on the world to act decisively. This was a global conjuncture that appears uniquely favourable to geopolitical cooperation. At the close of 1989, against the background of sweeping democratic change in Eastern Europe, President George Bush Sr and Soviet General Secretary Mikhail Gorbachev formally declared the Cold War over. But the intensely liberal, totemic qualities of 1989 were deceptive. The brand of liberalism globalizing in this moment was conservative, elitist and – crucially – rejected the notion that capitalist markets had to be subject to democratic regulation and control (see Chapter Two). Thus the state would be small, taxes low and capital as far as possible free of any democratic control.

How does the rise of authoritarian protectionism fit into this picture? It answers a demand for protection and recognition in societies that are experiencing intense disruption, crisis and change. It responds to anxieties and injustices with the false solidarity of exclusionary identity politics. Rather than addressing the structural causes of crisis, it finds respite in bitter grievance. According to this logic, the ethno-nation will be protected against the threats ranged against it – both phantom and real, and within or without the polity. This politics interacts with the economic structure of the world economy in a complex way. In a time of high inequality, it offers an elite politics in the guise of mass politics. So, it fits, in the Gramscian sense, with the 'demands of history' (Chapter Two), proposing an ethnonationalist 'togetherness' as an alternative to increasing demands for socioeconomic justice.

Neoliberalism has created a global system with very high levels of inequality. The structure that globalized in the 1990s favours the holders of assets over those dependent on wages (Piketty, 2014). Often regional inequalities, as opposed to individual or class-based inequality, have been key in animating support for the new authoritarian nationalists. 'Geographies of discontent' (Dijkstra et al, 2020), forming in small town, post-industrial settings, left vulnerable to competitive restructuring brough about by global trade and finance, have proven fertile territories for a politics based on racial and national grievance. But on the global level this is not the only dynamic at play. As we discussed in Chapter Two, the mobilizing techniques of Modi in India draws heavily upon aspirational, individualistic ideology. *Hindutva* is used in tandem with sub-national conceptions of the traditional caste system (Finnigan, 2019) to build a large following among aspirational middle classes attracted to his Islamophobia and racism. This is an authoritarian vision of an India rising by throwing off the weak and rewarding the strong. *Protection* is thus afforded to the deserving alone – an approach that has parallels with the tradition of racialized neoliberalism in Britain and the West, which also had a steep hostility to a lackadaisical underclass seen as deserving of their plight (Shilliam, 2018, 2020).

Authoritarianism in the long crisis has an amplification or spiral effect. It arises out of a failure of the existing system to establish an equitable and sustainable model of development. But it makes finding a route towards a more stable system much harder. While climate scientists have developed sophisticated models of the projected effects of global warming, until recently these had not incorporated the element of human political sociology, that is, the choices that societies make, which, in their combination, profoundly affect our common, ecological imprint. Since 2015, however, some climate models have included this through what scientists call 'Shared Socioeconomic Pathways' or SSPs (Tollefson, 2020). These build narrative timelines in which different political outlooks come to dominate the international system with distinct ecological effects. Although published a year prior to Brexit and Trump's election, one of these scenarios, SSP 3, 'Regional rivalry – a rocky road', assumed a world of heightened nationalism and drew ominous conclusions for the effect on climate change policy:

> [In SSP 3] concerns about economic competitiveness and security lead to trade wars. As the decades progress, national efforts to lock down energy and food supplies short-circuit global development. Investments in education and technology decline. Curbing greenhouse gases would be difficult in such a world, and adapting to climate change wouldn't be any easier. Under this scenario, the average global temperature is projected to soar to more than 4 °C above pre-industrial levels. (Tollefson, 2020)

There is, then, a sense of political tragedy in the relationship of authoritarian nationalism to the long crisis. For it is simultaneously present at the level of cause and effect; it arises out of the eroding of democratic authority, but once unleashed has a further amplification effect on ecological breakdown.

These crises occur, however, in the context of changed expectations for how states respond (on this see Barnett, 2020), which reflect new forms of cultural and economic organization. In previous long crises the authority drawn on by empires and kingdoms was founded on some kind of traditional claim to rulership. Contrastingly, in modern societies governments claim popular legitimacy. Even totalitarian states tend to derive a legal 'right to rule' from their populations – not, for the most part, from the individual sovereign claims of rulers or imperial traditions. Modern societies have a broad conception of the public interest, which means the remit of the state and its concept of protection is expansive. Schooling, health infrastructure, employment regulation, pension provision, social security, and so on, are a sign of societies that claim a legitimacy from their populations. This package of changes associated with the modern world have often been referred to as the creation of a mass society (Kornhauser, 2013; Arendt, 2019) where public authority is 'depersonalised', that is, not based on individual sovereigns ruling as a result of inherited tradition (Habermas, 1991). Over the last three centuries national identity became the glue in which rulers and ruled identified with one another in these new conditions of mass society. It provides an ever-present pool of feelings and emotions that frame the political field, and, thus, establishes a central prism through which any question of protection from crisis is understood.

The enduring power of national belonging

Seeing the 21st century as one defined by crisis and system-change confronts the following potential problem. Many have argued – correctly – that the extraordinary violence of the last century was unprecedented in human history. This is, after all, the central theme of Hobsbawm's *Age of Extremes*, which opens with a series of reflections on this very point: the scale of violence and suffering humanity had endured across this period. What he called the short 20th century ran from 1914 to the fall of the Soviet Union and was defined by an ideo-logical contest between different visions of the modern indus-trial world: liberalism, communism and fascism engaging in a fundamental and often extremely violent conflict. Hobsbawm's reflections on the role played by the concepts of *good and evil* in these battles actually speak strongly to the new ideologues of authoritarian protectionism. He warned that such moral contests are invoked by victors and vanquished alike to pros-ecute political struggle. 'This is one of the penalties of living through a century of religious wars', he wrote. 'Intolerance is their characteristic ... [they] did not think the world was big enough for permanent coexistence with rival secular religions' (Hobsbawm, 1995, p 5). This religious intolerance resurfaced swiftly after the fall of the Soviet Union but in a new form, no longer defined by utopian ideologies with competing visions for the 'final' stage of human civilization. Instead of this degen-erate utopianism, the ethnic and national identities we inherit from the past have largely defined the terms of the new good and evil. Indeed, in the first phase of the long 21st century, the 1990s, this possibility was posited as a clear warning: the appalling genocide in Rwanda and the terrible brutalities seen in the Yugoslavian wars illustrated the violent potential of a 'good and evil' that was defined according to national or ethnic identity. The varieties of authoritarian protectionism discussed in this book mobilize violence in less 'total' but still acute forms. They involve the same refusal of coexistence Hobsbawm warned against.

Hobsbawm himself was swift to anticipate the role that nationality would play in this 'new era' – and, indeed, it was a fact that perhaps could not be denied in the upsurge of demands for national self-determination which erupted with the fall of the Soviet Union. He saw it as reflecting an underlying desire *to belong*. When other solidarities fail nations are the community that are still present in our lives:

> But for those who can no longer rely on belonging anywhere else, there is at least one other imagined community to which one can belong: which is permanent, indestructible, and whose membership is certain. Once again 'the nation', or the ethnic group, 'appears as the ultimate guarantee' when society fails. You don't have to do anything to belong to it. You can't be thrown out. You are born in it and stay in it … And how do men and women know that they belong to this community? Because they can define the others who do not belong, who should not belong, who never can belong. In other words, by xenophobia. And because we live in an era when all other human relations and values are in crisis, or at least somewhere on a journey towards unknown and uncertain destinations, xenophobia looks like becoming the mass ideology of the 20th-century *fin de siècle*. What holds humanity together today is the denial of what the human race has in common. (Hobsbawm, 1992, pp 7–8)

Hobsbawm's remarks at the dawn of the long 21st century offer a prescient commentary on its development since. The demands for belonging and recognition appear to be a critical feature of this period, ones which are highly amenable to the core underlying imagination of human association: nationality. The centrality of nationalism and national identity in world affairs has a persistent quality across the 20th and 21st centuries alike – though not an unqualified one without countervailing tendencies. Indeed, these two phases of human development could be drawn together and viewed as part of a totality. We could speak of a longer period of time marked by crisis and instability, encompassing the 20th and 21st centuries and shaped by a reckoning between the social and ecological dimensions of industrialization (on this see Buzan and Lawson, 2015). Nations and nation-states were not simply empty shells in this long period of crisis and social transformation. They both formed the arenas for the struggles between the ideologies of the 20th century but also gave them distinct meanings in their own right. The concept of the 'national interest' has been, for example, ubiquitous throughout. Recognition of belonging and its inverse – xenophobia – provided a continuously available pool of images that were too visceral and institutionalized for either the liberals or the communists of the last century to challenge. Once their ideological and geopolitical conflict was over with the end of the Cold War, nationalism remained the undying thread of this longer span of time.

The rupture that occurs between the short 20th century and the long 21st does not therefore concern nationalism and national identity, which is a continuous component of this longer era. Rather it denotes the diminished status of 'utopian' horizons, whether reactionary or progressive. The appeal of nationalism once 'freed' from an attachment to a utopian vision lies in its focus on the past and present. Tradition, identity, culture and belonging are inherited from the past. The sense that this traditional order is somehow being lost or threatened animates nationalism's appeal. Authoritarian protectionism asserts itself into this cultural fabric. It is notable for its anti-utopianism, the narrowness of its horizon. In this regard, at least, it departs from the genocidal nightmare of interwar fascism that pledged to create through conquest a new world order based on racial purity. Even in the form of 'Xi Jinping Thought' (see Chapter Five) it promises to uphold the security and wellbeing of the people as they exist, not as they might be. The attachment to an egalitarian future is purely nominal. Xiism constitutes an ideology defined entirely by the metric of the Chinese struggle for greatness in the *existing* world.

Nonetheless, the relationship between authoritarian protectionism and nationality is dynamic and reciprocal, not absolute. Historically speaking, the process of inventing nation-states out of nations was often laced with violence. These territorial units were seen as the primary, if not exclusive, property of a dominant ethnonational group – and this defined the terms of national belonging and exclusion (on this see Valluvan, 2019, pp 39–48). But the fact this often occurred in the historical formation of nation-states does not make this an essential element of nationality. Nations, as cultural forms of association, are not 'programmed', so to speak, to aggressively pursue their own interests, define these in ethnically exclusive terms, and reject the idea of international cooperation. In other words, they are not preordained towards authoritarian protectionist narratives and goals. But the patchwork organization of societies into a world full of potentially conflicting claims – that is, the nation-state system, as such – does create an underlying social structure where ethnic nationalism is always present as a temptation.

This system is not without its limits and structural constraints. Neither does it enjoy an ahistorical permanence. The cultural frames and associations of nationality came into being at a particular moment in history and 'might conceivably give place to some other concept of human association' (White, 1975, pp 174–175). But it does appear to be a political identity distinctively fertile in this century and the last. Authoritarian protectionism builds upon the underlying cultural register of nationality. It harnesses the desire for belonging, activates its exclusionary potential and orientates it towards despotic aims. These are powerful weapons that can be mobilized to distract and channel public concern away from structural inequalities of power. Ethno-nationalism has often played this part admirably well throughout history, racializing issues of inequality, for example, through references to a supposedly corrupt Jewish elite, rather than substantive social and economic institutions or forces. Yet, national communities do not have to be defined in these racial and ethnic terms. And, we might argue, in fact, that the basic concept of equal participation in a community with a shared identity logically presumes an equitable and fair division of resources among citizens. In other words, national solidarities may be – and, indeed, *have been* – drawn on to support institutions, such as the British National Health Service, that assume citizens have a shared responsibility to the wellbeing of each other.

From 'I won't protect you' to 'I will protect you'?

There are, in short, different possibilities in how the concept of national protection can be defined. It is a subject of immense actual and potential contestation, which raises the issue of how to render support for international cooperation, and with it the notion of a universal or general interest, consistent with the fact of humanity's separation into different societies and communities. In International Relations, this has been discussed in terms of uneven and combined development (Rosenberg, 2006; Anievas, 2014) and interactive multiplicity (Kurki and Rosenberg, 2020). This idea starts from the basic observation that the world is divided into many different polities, each with distinct economic capabilities, cultural traditions, institutions and ethnic composition. Differences between societies imparts unevenness and variation to the nature of human development. Individual societies are also, however, shaped by their interaction or 'combination' with one another. They encounter shared problems and realities. They may compete through dynamic innovation, taking advantage of the circulation of ideas to adapt techniques pioneered elsewhere to national circumstances. But may also engage in predatory, beggar-thy-neighbour competition, seeking sectional advantage and rejecting global cooperation. States will often mediate between these extremes, pursuing neither wholly self-interested nor universal outcomes. These will reflect the ideological divisions within their own domestic politics, which are, in turn, also shaped by the outside world. But even those with the strongest attachment to an internationalist approach will still, to some degree, frame their outlook in terms of national protection.

Protection is therefore an important animating theme for how contemporary states respond to crisis conditions in the international system. While it can be given either a progressive or regressive content, the notion of protection as having a value for the community is nonetheless usually recognized, even if cast in different language (such as 'security'). Some far right thinkers in the Anglosphere do, however, theoretically reject the concept of a 'state that protects'. This is distinct from a politician that fails to deliver on their commitment to protection. It instead derogates from the very idea. This 'Dark Enlightenment' school has grown in prominence in recent years with the rise in support for the radical right. It is associated with individuals such as the PayPal founder, Peter Thiel, and the alt-right pseudointellectuals, Nick Land and Curtis Yarvin. A highly reactionary form of 'accelerationist' philosophy (which also has its leftist variants – such as the work of the late Mark Fisher), it advocates maximum disruption to the status quo through sweeping technological transformation based on releasing capitalism, as far as possible, from any kind of constraint (for a discussion of this school of thought see Runciman, 2018, chapter 4; Mason, 2019, chapter 6). Social or human protection in any form is therefore attacked by this thinking on the grounds that it seeks to inhibit the reproduction of capitalism.

This alt-right group hold democracy itself to constitute a dangerous block on acceleration. In a widely cited 2009 blog post, Thiel argued that he no longer believed democracy was compatible with his libertarian economic political philosophy. He lamented how the fallout from the 2008 financial crisis had created a new state-dependent economics. 'Those who have argued for free markets have been [left] screaming into a hurricane' (Thiel, 2009), he wrote. In the same post, he argued that the expansion of the franchise to women and the creation of the welfare state had generated forces that would destroy economic freedom – only a handbrake turn away from democratic government could save it (Thiel, 2009).

Similar themes are also found in the output of Yarvin. 'Americans [are] going to have to get over their dictator phobia', as he has put it (cited in Pein, 2018, np). Only authoritarian rule, either in the form of a neo-reactionary monarchy or a corporate-style executive government, would be able to protect the economic freedoms of capitalism from corrosive democratic demands. Yarvin has also been credited with introducing the alt-right 'red pill' meme (Yarvin, 2019). Referring to the Matrix film franchise, the idea was initially taken up in the 'manosphere', an online community in which taking the red pill denotes a sudden awakening to a new reality of a world dominated by liberal and feminist values, but later morphed into a broader alt-right symbol – with Ivanka Trump among its acolytes. As this suggests, despite their futurist, tech-heavy language, this milieu's ideas tend to simply resuscitate classic far right perspectives. They embrace, for example, highly racialized, social-Darwinist thinking, typical of the 19th-century West, but in seemingly anodyne or obtuse language. As Corey Pein observes, their support for a 'human biodiversity' agenda, which simply rehashes the age-old lie of Black intellectual inferiority, amounts to little more than 'racism in a lab coat' (Pein, 2018, np).[1] Protection of the environment is also condemned in frenzied and authoritarian terms. In one long, rambling blog post, for instance, discussing the alleged takeover of society by a scientific elite, Yarvin even argued that the eminent climate scientist Michael E. Mann 'should be in prison' (Yarvin, 2009).

If one could summarize this school of thought in a single term it might simply be: 'I won't protect you'. It is a survival of the fittest vision of society based upon a racialized hyper-competition within capitalism. All bonds of human and environmental community are seen as the enemy to the techno-march of history. Thiel's opposition to the enfranchisement of women is revealing given the masculinized vision of the world offered by the Dark Enlightenment movement: great men will rise to dominate both women and other men. They would destroy all ecological barriers to acceleration in this Promethean vision. Thus the strong would prosper. The weak would stand crushed in history's march.

Yet, this underlying alt-right philosophy was modified significantly when it touched political reality. On the one hand, it undoubtedly influenced Trump's approach to government. His one-time advisor Steve Bannon, for example, has spoken of the need to 'deconstruct the administrative state', a minimal state being an important touchstone principle for this group of economic libertarians (Michaels, 2017; see also Chapter Five). On the other hand, in public the extreme free market agenda has been carefully downplayed. Thiel's 2016 Republican Convention is a case in point. His endorsement of Trump said nothing of his own libertarianism. It stuck totally to the script of the 'leftist' campaign:

'Where I work in Silicon Valley it's hard to see where American has gone wrong. My industry has made a lot of progress in computers and in software. And, of course, it's made a lot of money. But Silicon Valley is a small place. Drive out to Sacramento or even across the bridge to Oakland and you won't see the same prosperity … Across the country wages are flat, Americans get paid less today than ten years ago but healthcare and college tuition cost more every year. Meanwhile, Wall Street bankers inflate everything from government bonds to Hilary's Clinton's speakers' fees. Our economy is broken.' (Thiel, 2016)

In other words, the message was simple: Donald Trump will protect you, deliver true prosperity to you and your family and restore your pride in the United States of America. In a quite stunning piece of political opportunism, democracy's intellectual opponents had suddenly found their democratic voice.

In a blink of an eye, 'I won't protect you' was transformed itself into 'I will'. Thiel's speech can be read, in this regard, as a short illustration of how the idea of protection in a time of crisis has this catchall appeal. As societies face a series of crises, real insecurities combining with the frenzied fears of the collective imagination, populations will judge politicians according to their capacity to protect.

Opponents of democracy can always declare themselves the people's champions

The anti-democratic thinkers on the new alt-right can be situated within a broader intellectual tradition of capitalist authoritarianism – or conservative, pro-market, anti-democratic liberalism. Nineteenth-century liberals fretted that democracy in the form of universal suffrage would imperil property rights as populations might choose to legislate for the abolition of capitalism. So, they opposed both absolutism, or 'feudalistic' structures of authority, and the mass democratic franchise in equal measure. David Hume's conception of a 'well-tempered democracy' was, for instance, limited to 'all men of any property or means' (McArthur, 2007, p 76). Even the more democratically orientated reformers often had 'mixed feelings' (Hinde, 1987, p 42) about the expansion of the franchise. Mill, who was in many respects one of the more progressive figures within this intellectual tradition (see Chapter Two), also advocated a franchise system that granted different numbers of votes according to professional employment (Mill, 2019; see also Runciman, 2018, chapter 4). Even before the 21st-century new right, this anti-democratic thinking was recovered by liberals that were sympathetic to the Chilean military junta of Augusto Pinochet and advised the regime on its free market reforms (Fischer, 2009).

The fact authoritarianism and democracy observes a pendulum-like motion in history, moving in waves between one pole and the other, reflects tensions that are perhaps fundamental to the idea of democracy itself. In the broad sweep of history, organizing societies democratically is still a relatively novel exercise. Universal suffrage in competitive elections, a key tenet of formal democracy, required the expansion of the electorate to women and the non-property-holding working classes – something that has only been practised on a wide scale since the beginning of the 20th century. It also necessitated the break-up of the old colonial empires, which were inherently antithetical to democracy – a process that only began in earnest after the Second World War. So, in contrast to David Runciman's musing that democracy may be experiencing a 'midlife crisis' (Runciman, 2018), we might argue, in light of this still relatively compressed history, that the travails facing democratic systems of government all over the world may simply express the ongoing birth pangs of its historical awakening.

Although democracy's strength lies in its ability to move flexibly between different policies and preferences, the frenzy for free markets and technocracy that broke out in the 1990s underlined the ease with which *formal* democratic mechanisms could fail to deliver *substantively* democratic outcomes. Shifts in policies favouring different groups and classes are not therefore free of power relations. On the contrary, we have seen on countless occasions how wealth can bring huge influence over the democratic process. In this sense, while democracy is infinitely better than dictatorship, it contains an inevitable struggle between different interest groups – and these rival blocs do not contest the game as equals. Universal suffrage provides one vote for all, but in substance some individuals and factions have much more power than others. Recognizing this reality leads to what Mouffe has referred to as the 'agonistic' model of democracy, which accepts there is no 'perfect harmony or transparency' possible (Mouffe, 2009, p 100). Rather the formal and substantive aspects of democracy have to be continually fought for, as no perfect institutional settlement exists that can establish them 'for all time'.

Seen in these terms we should not perhaps be surprised about the rebirth of struggle between democracy and authoritarianism. For democracy as an idea has huge normative power; and this means those engaged in eroding both the formal and substantive elements of it will nonetheless often declare their commitment to the idea that 'the people' (*dêmos*) do and must hold power (*krátos*). The extreme form this has taken with the American alt-right, combining philosophical musings on the need to end democracy with rhetorical appeals to championing the democratic collective, encapsulates a problem Jacques Derrida warned against. Democracy as an idea, he argued, contains the deep contradiction that its substantive opponents can always play the linguistic game of declaring themselves democrats (Derrida, 2005, p 31). And in times of crisis and disfunction they can find ample opportunity to do so.

Today we can observe this playing out as authoritarians march under democracy's banner.

FOUR

Pandemic Politics

For us, this is a crisis and a big test.

*Xi Jinping, after a meeting with
Cabinet and officials, February 2020*

This is the reality: the virus is there. We have to face it, but face it like a man, damn it, not like a kid. We'll confront the virus with reality. That's life. We're all going to die one day.

*Jair Bolsonaro, speaking during a tour
of suburbs in Brasilia, March 2020*

COVID-19 can be seen as an overwhelming singularity for the entire world; a force from which no society can escape. This draws immediate comparison to other breakdowns in the relationship to nature which we find in long crises across centuries and even millennia of human development. History is full of warnings of how events in the ecosphere interacted with the human world to generate extreme breakdowns. The crises of the 14th and 17th centuries drove changes in the socioeconomic and institutional organization of societies across the globe. This modernization was, itself, a violent process involving intense struggle between classes and states, which overlay the hardship brought about by the changing ecological context. Yet, viewed in retrospect, it is still possible to discern some sense of scientific and other forms of social progress within this long pattern of historical change. But different cases of long crises offer more dire warnings of the potentials for eco-driven system breakdown. A compelling example is the Late Bronze Age collapse. In the first half of the 12th century BC, the civilizations of the interconnected regional system encompassing the Eastern Mediterranean, Aegean and Western Asia all collapsed. They included the Egyptian empire, the Kassites of Babylonian, the Mycenaean kingdoms of Greece, and the Hittites whose empire centred on Anatolia. Climate change, producing severe, generalized drought, has been identified as an underlying environmental condition. These fractures in the human ecology prompted socioeconomic crises in what were, at the time, some of the most advanced societies on Earth (Kaniewski et al, 2010; Drake, 2012). Like in our own era, however, these ecological conditions interpenetrate with causal dynamics arising from the social world. Although much of the history of this period remains unknown (see Knapp and Manning, 2016 for scepticism of the climactic cause) scholars have ventured the hypothesis that, as political and economic institutions were unable to reorganize in the face of famine-induced economic downturn, the crises took on a 'multiplier effect' (for a survey, see Cline, 2015, pp 161–165), where human social responses aggravated the environmental breakdown, driving the civilizations in the region to total destruction.

There are, of course, limits in the extent to which we can draw parallels between the relatively mysterious Late Bronze Age collapse and the ecological and social crises of this century. But the possibilities of multiplier effects that aggravate the underlying condition of social and ecological distress eerily resonate with our own era. Authoritarian protectionism has this spiral quality to it. A broken global economic order forms one part of the long crisis of this century that its ideological rise tends to accelerate, taking disparities in income to even higher levels. And in relation to the two other dimensions – the breakdown in global governance and the underlying crisis in the relationship to natural world – the pattern is similar.

Authoritarian protectionists do not all need to follow Trump's climate change denialism, which has led to a sweeping offensive against environmental regulation and the championing of fossil fuel (Gross, 2020), in order to present a severe problem to climate change efforts. The simple posture of aggressively prioritizing the ethno-nation over the general interest presents an acute problem for the cooperative and global effort needed to undertake a sustainable transition.

The 21st-century long crisis: the ecological conditions driving pandemic politics

The severe famines that played a role in the Late Bronze Age collapse were primarily events of ecological contingency. Low productivity agriculture was inherently vulnerable to such contingent shifts in ecological conditions, though demands to increase output with population growth may also have contributed to pressure on the land. But the social imprint of human activity is much more profound when it comes to the industrial and post-industrial age we are living through. In this era of the Anthropocene, the point in human history in which our collective imprint on planet Earth decisively transforms its material nature, environmental events will often entail causes drawn from human relations. Indeed, COVID-19 has even been referred to as the 'disease of the Anthropocene'. It reflects an epochal moment in which humanity is 'transforming the earth's natural habitats and ecosystems by intensely altering the patterns and mechanisms of interaction between species', creating new opportunities for the cultivation and transmission of diseases from animals to humans (O'Callaghan-Gordo and Antó, 2020). In its origins and spread through the human ecology COVID-19 exposes vulnerabilities in how we have come to live in the 21st century, how we feed ourselves, and how we connect with one another.

Politics does not just determine the way in which the virus spread through the global system. It also establishes through policy and institutions the matrix of social and environmental conditions creating localities that are susceptible to the transmission of viral pathogens from animals to humans. 'Locality', as Rob Wallace argues in *Big Farms Make Big Flu*, 'has meaning beyond where the pathogen happened to originate', because 'public policy and social practice', that is, politics and institutions, shape the ecologies in which diseases arise and spread (Wallace, 2016, p 28). Wallace's book is highly critical of the Chinese and American resistance to dealing effectively with pathogen risk in their meat production supply chains. He notes how the former has adopted industrial farming techniques from the latter and applied them on a very large scale domestically. At the same time, China has also become a meat importer firmly locked into the globalization of the food supply system.

This context has led to the overall heightening of pandemic risk. Indeed, the specific biological origins of COVID-19 reflect the particular symbiosis of Sino-American uneven and combined development in this century. China's drive to industrialize and 'catch up' with the United States has involved creating a US-style meat industry. The history of Shuanghui Group, which rebranded itself as WH Group in 2014, following its takeover of American meat production giant, Smithfield Foods, illustrates these connections and the peculiarities of China's history. The company started life as an enterprise set up by the Luohe city government in 1958, just as Mao's China was about to embark on the 'Great Leap Forward', a disastrous experiment in agricultural collectivization, decentralized industrial production and uncoordinated planning by so-called 'People's Communes'. Some six decades later, and following the country's remarkably successful turn to capitalist industrial modernization in 1979, the firm had become the largest pork company in the world with a listing on the Hong Kong Stock Exchange. Global investors have tended to look positively at the East Asian market for growth in global meat production. Rising middle-class consumption patterns have transformed meat products from a one-time luxury commodity to a regular part of many East Asian diets – a trend that is expected to continue. But the industrial farming methods employed in this expansion have brought considerable pressures onto the ecosystem. Moreover, the role these techniques have played in increasing global pandemic risk is still hardly discussed. Despite the severity of the COVID-19 crisis, it remains almost totally overlooked.

Global debate has often focused on the role of East Asia's traditional 'wet markets' in creating environments favour-able to pathogens spreading from humans to animals. These are conurbations of small traders in urban environments selling meats and fish that are killed on site, rather than at slaughterhouses. By increasing contact with live animals these markets do create opportunities for viruses to move from livestock to humans. At the start of the COVID-19 crisis attention immediately focused on the Huanan Seafood Wholesale Market, which was closed permanently by the Chinese authorities on 1 January 2020. In late February, the Chinese government followed this up with a complete ban on 'wet markets' across the entire territory of the country. While this was probably a sensible measure, the danger of focusing on 'wet markets' is that it ignores the role of industrial farming in increasing the pathogen transmission risk from animals to humans. In fact, the Chinese authorities have had a longer-term preference to move away from wet markets, as well as smaller-scale production, as part of their active support for an Americanized model of meat production and distribution.

A 2014 report highlighted the danger that Chinese policy 'singled out' wet markets 'as a major source of disease epidemics; while "specialized" producers, much smaller and weaker than the firms that contract with them, are being blamed for food safety issues' (Pi et al, 2014, pp 30–31). It also noted how China had converged on a US style system, in which the total focus on profit was creating a 'race to the bottom' culture that undermined workers' safety and public health. These methods involve the massive concentration of birds within cramped conditions, creating hotbeds of disease transmission, and leading, in turn, to the overuse of antibiotics and additives to keep the birds alive (Pi et al, 2014, pp 28–30). In the EU, most American poultry is banned due to the widespread use of anti-microbial chemical washes ('chlorinated chicken'). While the use of chlorine is not, in itself, seen as a dangerous, it compensates for the very poor welfare conditions that poultry are kept in, which then requires the use of chemical washes to disinfect disease-ridden meat. Researchers have also found these methods to be ineffective in eliminating pathogens, underlining the risks of this approach (Highmore et al, 2018).

Another prescient report written for global investors in the Asian farm and livestock market, which, as such, is unlikely to have a strong bias towards trade justice and animal welfare campaigners, highlighted significant public health risks arising from the turn to large-scale factory farming:

> There are major public health risks associated with the livestock sectors in the [Asian] markets covered by this report. There is increasingly compelling evidence that overuse of antibiotics in livestock production is contributing to the growth of antibiotic resistant bacteria in humans and animals. This could make many common diseases and infections untreatable ... At the same time, viral infections and livestock epidemics are increasing in frequency and severity with strains of avian and swine flu a key concern. These can result in significant livestock culls. For example, more than 35 million birds were culled in South Korea during 2016/2017, which depressed prices and lowered demand for the product. (Farm Animal Investment Risk and Return, 2017, p 7)

Pandemic risk will be a crucial issue for capitalist investment decisions in the post- COVID-19 world. If the spread of new pathogens endangering human life is becoming more common, then it raises question for all businesses, large and small, about how to calculate and manage risk. For big corporates, however, the current system has an easy remedy to protect their interests: extensive state subsidy of investors with the profits remaining firmly privatized. In the 2013 Avian flu outbreak, for example, the Chinese state provided 600 million yuan (the equivalent of around US$97 million) to support the poultry industry as the authorities carried out large culls of infected livestock (Pi et al, 2014, p 24). Demand for meat has also remained high through the economic shock of COVID-19. Even though the industry may have played a role in creating conditions favourable to the transfer of pathogens from animals to humans, they are not directly exposed to the risk of this happening. So, the risks and incentives in play are all wrong.

How we choose to feed ourselves is one eco-social driver of the new pandemic politics. The other is the human-crafted environments in which we live. As Mike Davis has argued in his remarkably prescient book, *The Monster at the Door*, warning of global pandemics from animal pathogens (re-published in 2020 as *The Monster Enters*), the sociological structure of contemporary human civilization is almost perfectly designed to facilitate transmission (Davis, 2020). Capitalist production embedded within geographical ecologies has created what he calls 'structures of disease emergence' (Davis, 2020, np). Deforestation, whether driven by capitalist agricultural farms or subsistence producers, leads to biodiversity loss, creating new opportunities for animal–human contact. Profit-based logics in pharmaceuticals and healthcare provision drive the overuse of antibiotics, undermining microbial resistance. Cramped human living conditions, from slums to cityscapes, create mass urban incubation units for the cultivation and transmission of pathogens. These sociological realities of modern living represent a perfect storm of forces favourable to the generation of potentially deadly contagions.

None of these conditions can be easily reformed out of existence. They posit – as Davis emphasizes – the need for revolutionary change in the social relations that embed human societies in the ecosphere in a more sustainable way. And changes of this order will, naturally, not come about overnight. No millenarian rupture can be expected. Instead it suggests a horizon of change operating firmly on the longer span of time, one navigating the systemic breakdowns of the 21st century. These attempts to find new pathways will have to contend with the challenges posed by humanity's organizational and cultural complexity; the way we live our lives in a polycentric web of separate yet continuously interacting national communities. Indeed, this seems like one of the most basic realities that COVID-19 illustrated as it moved through the international system in 2020. For all the integration of the globalized world, cultural, political and institutional differences from one society to the next, have profoundly shaped how the pandemic spread from human to human across the world.

COVID-19 has had vastly different impacts on the world's populations

The global political system was poorly prepared for the pandemic. Since 2008 it had already been fracturing under the pressures of rising nationalism and political authoritarianism. But it did at least have a system of global governance capable of coordination and knowledge sharing. Through 2020 the World Health Organization (WHO) would attempt to move a crisis-wracked multilateral system in a cooperative direction. When it declared a 'Public Health Emergency of International Concern' on 30 January 2020, the world's nation-states had a small window of opportunity to act decisively to contain and eliminate the pandemic. Many did so. But with no vaccine they were still, collectively, at the mercy of those that did not. No country could feel safe while the virus remained in global circulation.

In epidemiological terms, COVID-19 was the nightmare scenario. Highly contagious, potentially deadly but with large numbers of asymptomatic carriers making containment particularly difficult. An incubation period of up to 14 days, the time in which the virus is present but had not reached a threshold in the carrier to show up in tests or prompt symptoms, added further to these problems. Many countries, particularly in the West where an underlying cultural sense of supremacy over the rest of the world has somehow persisted in defiance of the East Asian economic ascent, were complacent and slow to act. In countries that had a relatively painless experience of the previous global viruses, such as SARS (2002–2004), Ebola (ongoing since the 1970s but particularly in West Africa, 2013–2016) and Swine flu (2009), governments often lulled themselves into a false sense of security and failed to prepare.

COVID-19 would spread through the international system in a very uneven form. Some countries have been crippled by the virus; others would see a relatively swift return to something approaching 'normal'. In August 2020, a video was repeatedly shared through global social media that showed young revellers in Wuhan, China, the initial ground zero for the outbreak, enjoying a pool party. In the United States, in the same month, cases were still rising by an order of magnitude in the tens of thousands every day; such that by 1 September 2020 the country had recorded six million infections. China's strict quarantine had succeeded while America and the rest of the world faced tumult and chaos.

What accounts for this spectacular difference in the impact of COVID-19? While the spread of viruses can be conditioned by local climatological contexts, in the case of COVID-19 'the social world', that is, collective human behaviour, specifically the policies that states pursue, their institutional capacity to deliver on them, and their relationship to broader society, has been the critically decisive factors.

The way COVID-19 ripped through the global system, with the pattern of contagion determined almost wholly by each state's response, provides a striking illustration of how global development has this uneven and combined character: how states used the sovereignty at their disposal in this politically fractured world shaped how the virus spread through the international system. By August 2020, for instance, there were a mere ten countries that had not recorded a single case of COVID-19 (Amos, 2020).[1] All located in the island archipelagos of Oceania, their governments had virtually shut off contact with the outside world to protect their citizens from the virus. But their tourist, fishing and remittances-dependent economies were crippled by the lockdown. So, despite their national quarantine, these states still felt the whirlwind of global forces 'at home', even if the form this took was an economic depression, not their exposure to the deadly impact of the COVID-19 pandemic.

On 25 February 2020, nearly a month after the WHO had announced its emergency protocol, the crisis was beginning to spike but was still largely located in East Asia. Eighty thousand cases had been positively identified with 97 per cent of these in China. The WHO's Assistant Director, Bruce Aylward, warned that immediate and decisive action was now critical. 'The single biggest lesson [from China]', he remarked, is 'speed is everything' (in Cohen, 2020). He expressed concern that the rest of the world was failing to observe this principle (Cohen, 2020). A few days later the WHO published a report of a joint eight-day mission with the Chinese state to review the state of the pandemic. The implications for the rest of the world could not have been clearer. They described the virus as 'a new pathogen that is *highly contagious*, can spread quickly, and must be considered capable of causing *enormous* health, economic and societal impacts in any setting' (World Health Organization, 2020a, p 18, emphasis added). 'It is not', they warned, challenging international complacency, 'SARS and it is not influenza' (World Health Organization, 2020a, p 18).

The report praised the achievements of the Chinese state in bringing the outbreak under control. China is, of course, an economically powerful, industrialized economy. But with no known treatment or vaccine, containing the virus in spring

2020 depended on 'old fashioned' anti-contagion techniques, particularly quarantine and contact-tracing among the infected. The ability to mobilize and organize state resources rapidly and efficiently was critical to stopping the spread of the disease.

The WHO report described how the Chinese authorities had implemented 'a policy of meticulous case and contact identification' with 'more than 1800 teams of epidemiologists, with a minimum of 5 people/team ... tracing tens of thousands of contacts a day' (World Health Organization, 2020a, p 8). These were then followed up through a programme of laboratory testing to identify confirmed cases. In tandem with this a strict lockdown, including sweeping closures to public life, was introduced across the whole of China. In Hubei province, home to the Wuhan epicentre, the lockdown was even more severe with public transport systems suspended and support teams created, ferrying food and supplies to households to allow them to remain indoors under the strict quarantine system.

China's authoritarian, one-party state system proved highly effective in its capacity to mobilize and direct public resources. The quite extreme level of shutdown in Hubei mitigated the extent of the spread in China and provided the rest of the world with vital time. Replicating the extent of the lockdown China pursued was either beyond the capacity of many states or, at least in the 'total lockdown' form assumed in Hubei, considered an undesirable level of coercion. But the adoption of an analogous prevention method combining some form of lockdown quarantine and contact-tracing was within the capacity of most states globally. It did not ultimately require significant levels of wealth or a high-tech pharmaceutical industry. Indeed, the less a state could *afford* an uncontrolled outbreak due to limited healthcare capacity, the greater the incentive they had to move swiftly and early with low-cost measures.

Although practised in an authoritarian form by the Chinese authorities, democratic states could – and many did – pursue a response based on the professional organization and direction of state institutions using mass testing and contact-tracing. The

WHO could not have been clearer on the implications for the rest of the world at the end of February. They advocated adopting a Chinese-style model with 'uncompromising and rigorous use of non-pharmaceutical measures to contain transmission of the COVID-19 virus in multiple settings' (World Health Organization, 2020a, p 19). The WHO report effectively laid down a gauntlet to every government in the world: act swiftly now, or pay later.

COVID-19 represented in this sense a remarkable test of individual state institutional capacity and political traditions: the ability of political systems to respond effectively to an extreme social crisis. As states reacted in different ways to the challenge the virus posed it illustrated starkly the international character of the human world. For when the human species faced this threat it did not do so as a single collective, but separated out into a myriad of different societies, each with their own traditions, identities and institutions. The results of the 'test' posed to the nation-states of Earth were profound: radically different rates of infection and death rates became closely correlated with how governments individually responded. It laid bare the world's political, socioeconomic and institutional unevenness.

The world is not flat: COVID-19 forces us to ask questions about 'the best life'

The globalized system of the 21st century is certainly not – as was once alleged – 'flat' (Friedman, 2007; for a critique, see Christopherson et al, 2008). Rather than converging on the same development path, the world system is full of variation, despite being highly integrated. Neither has the playing field of global competition *flattened*. A large part of this 'flat Earth' account of globalization seemed to be based on the observation of elites in the global cities of this century; and here its one-sided conclusion was founded upon a kernel of truth. From monotonous high-rise architectural landscapes to the ultra-affluent clubs and bars of the metropolis, a certain life-world of the rich and affluent formed with the rise of globalization that gives the appearance of 'flatness'. Globalized, big finance created 'masters of the universe' (Jones, 2014), elite networks promoting a vision of how to organize capitalism in which investors could be set free from the constraints of space and even time. Financialization meant that tomorrow's profits could be cashed today. Meanwhile this politics successfully opened up the world to fast-moving money. But far from creating convergence this neoliberal globalism gave rise to something more akin to 'integrated divergence'. Globalization did not break free of the unevenness of human geography (Leamer, 2007) or the structural complexity of capitalism (Rosenberg, 2003). In fact, its transformative effects remained predicated on these realities.

When information, goods and commodities raced around the world these flows were actually shaped, mediated and filtered by the unevenness of the human condition. Investment capital freed from regulation and the constraints of national borders actually took advantage of this unevenness as it spread through the international system; lower labour costs, for example, spurred the 'sweat shop' outsourcing revolution. Individual states also competed to offer the most advantageous investment terms. While this exerted downward pressure ('the race to the bottom') on the conditions faced by global labour, the end result was still not wholesale conformity but divergence. Not all states were willing to play the globalization game in the same way. 'Hold out' states resisted the drive to total deregulation, governing according to different ideological principles, often reflecting their populations' demands. Neither did all states have the same resources to start with. No matter how intense competition became there was never the 'flattening' or level playing field that proponents of globalization claimed would result. The world would actually remain characterized by the opposite: a multi-layered, non-flatness. Globalization was at each stage in its developments structured by the uneven and combined interactions of societies with different models of governance, often based on distinct ideological and cultural traditions.

These structures, both cultural and institutional, have found themselves 'tested' by the COVID-19 pandemic. The governance exam seems close to what Greek philosopher Aristotle had in mind when he asked, 'what form of political community' allows individuals to 'realize their ideal of life', or 'the best life' (Aristotle, 350 BC). Aristotle cast this as an investigation into imperfection, not ideals, 'we only undertake this inquiry because all the constitutions with which we are acquainted are faulty' (Aristotle, 350 BC). The remark seem well suited to the test that COVID-19 has posed to the world's states. For there is a striking absence of perfection in today's crisis, which seems like the antithesis of the hubris seen in past moments of transition in international systems. Indeed, it radically challenges the elite narrative that dominated the last 'epochal' shift: the revolutions of 1989 and the consequent spread of liberalism and democracy. The dominant assumption of that conjuncture – which hailed the West as the 'winner' and declared its system should be mimicked by the rest of the world (on this see Appadurai, 2020) – now looks absurd. And the core foundation of this claim – that the rich world knew best and the poor should learn – equally breaks apart. The early results of the COVID-19 exam do not map neatly onto the rich/poor divide. Neither are there exemplar societies for the rest of the world to follow, even if some models of authoritarian governance have, as we will see, clearly emerged with greater legitimacy.

America and Britain, as the exemplars of the 'flat Earth' ideology, stand out in this regard. Pankaj Mishra, in his polemical indictment of these 'flailing states' published in the *London Review of Books*, finds in COVID-19 the ultimate historical comeuppance for 'these prime movers of modern civilisation' (Mishra, 2020). The Anglo-American vision of limited government, free markets and individual self-betterment – once compellingly described as 'the Lockean heartland', in reference to the liberal English philosopher, John Locke (van der Pijl, 2012) – is particularly poorly suited to the world brought into being by COVID-19. When British Prime Minister Boris Johnson said of his reluctance to move to a life-saving lockdown, 'we live in a land of liberty' (*BBC News*, 2020c), he expressed the natural ruling ethos of many among the Atlanticist elite: that the continued operation of the market was sacrosanct, whatever the costs to human life. His government's related, disastrous initial policy – 'herd immunity', the idea a 60 per cent rate of infection would provide sufficient immunity to the infection in the population as a whole – formed an equally organic application of the brutalities of neoliberal individualism to the pandemic: that the strong would pull through, even if the weak fell by the wayside.

COVID-19 posited the need for an entirely different governing philosophy. States had to effectively reconstruct themselves as highly centralized coordinators of society: closing down whole sectors, prioritizing essential services, providing large-scale state assistance to protect employment, opening new field hospitals, and systematically managing activity between the public and private sector in order to protect the general interest. A society's ability to do this is not, of course, entirely unrelated to its material wealth. Very poor and conflict-affected societies, in which the state lacks institutionalization and is the subject of rentier claims by elites (what Alex de Waal calls political marketplace societies, see de Waal, 2015) have very limited capacity to do this. Highly impoverished states that are not experiencing violent conflict are also likely to lack the health services to protect populations from the virus. This is starkly illustrated, for example, by the numbers of doctors per 10,000 people in poor states. Afghanistan has 2.8 doctors per 10,000 citizens, Sudan has 2.6, and the Democratic Republic of Congo has a mere 0.7. By contrast, the healthcare capacity of the world's wealthier states are in an altogether different league. Britain has 28 doctors per 10,000, the United States 26, Ireland 28, and Germany and Switzerland both have 42 (World Health Organization, 2020b). These vastly different resources are a huge advantage in tackling COVID-19. While the Solomon Islands, Micronesia and the Marshall Islands, all part of the group of 'zero COVID' Pacific island states, are desperately poor, they took the decision to close their borders to the outside world, knowing that their national health systems would struggle to cope in a pandemic situation. Their ability to do this is fairly exceptional vis-à-vis other very poor states.

Nonetheless, perhaps what is most striking about the early results of the test that COVID-19 presented to the world's societies is how material wealth has not proven to be as decisive a factor in a country's ability to contain the virus as might have been predicted. While absolute poverty remains a serious barrier to effective pandemic control and prevention, a number of middle-income states are highly institutionalized and have shown that they have the state capacity to fight COVID-19 effectively.

Consider the case of Vietnam, a one-party communist state still officially described as a 'Socialist Republic', despite decades of capitalist reform, beginning with the *Đổi Mới* ('Renovation') turn of 1986. According to conventional measures of economic and social wellbeing, Vietnam is not a rich country. The Human Development Index, for example, provides a statistical measure of social and economic wellbeing, including not only per capita national income but access to education and life expectancy. It places Vietnam in the middle of the table at 118 with what is described as a 'median' level of human development (United Nations Development Programme, 2019, p 301). This might imply that the country would be badly hit by the COVID-19 pandemic, without the resources to mobilize an effective public response to the pandemic. But Vietnam's record in containing the virus is exemplary by any global standard. According to the Johns Hopkins University, Vietnam first reported cases of COVID-19 on 23 January 2020. But as of 24 August 2020 it had registered just

27 deaths from the virus with 1,016 infections (Johns Hopkins University Coronavirus Resource Centre, 2020).

The country moved swiftly to lockdown to prevent the virus spreading, placed tens of thousands of individuals in state quarantine facilities and rapidly increased its testing capacity, rising from three laboratory facilities in January to 112 by the end of April 2020 (Vu et al, 2020). By the end of August it had performed over one million tests (Vietnamese Government, 2020), giving it a test to confirmed case ratio of around 1 to 1,000. By contrast, the UK, a stronghold of the global pharmaceutical industry and home to some of the world's leading universities for scientific research, suffered from a serious lack of testing capacity in spring 2020. And this meant its total number of COVID-19 cases were badly understated at the height of the pandemic. But, even with this caveat, the comparison is still remarkable. By the end of August its equivalent ratio was just 45 tests for every one confirmed infection (UK Government, 2020).

Vietnam's success in tackling COVID-19 through coordinated state intervention is a striking accomplishment in a country of over 95 million people, amounting to just 11 infections per million people. Compare this to the United States, still the world's strongest economy, which as of 1 September 2020 had 18,281 infections per million (Johns Hopkins University Coronavirus Resource Centre, 2020). By February 2021, the pandemic would still be ripping through the country's population. Many Western states experienced the debilitating effects of a 'second wave' across the winter months having failed to use the window of opportunity in the summer to radically drive down infection levels. The ingredients of the Vietnamese response are simple to discern. It has an institutionalized one-party state, with an authoritarian law and order system capable of coercively imposing discipline on its citizenry; an experience of dealing with previous viruses that have impacted East and South East Asia; a population that was, accordingly, respectful of the dangers of pandemics; and a very high incentive for the public health system not to be overwhelmed. With eight doctors per 10,000 citizens (World Health Organization, 2020b), Vietnam is a typical middle income country with a health infrastructure that could struggle to cope if containment failed and the viral contagion was unleashed on the country's population.

We can see, then, how state-level politics – from institutional capacity to specific government decisions – has had a tremendous impact in shaping the spread of the pandemic through the international system. Each state can, in this respect, be seen as a nodal point in the ecological and social structure of humanity as a whole. Actions taken by an individual state within this uneven and combined totality condition the way in which the virus spreads through the international system. But its interconnected character means that no state can be truly 'free' of the virus until all states take effective action. This has a clear parallel with the other environmental challenges the human species faces in this century. To avoid catastrophic global warming all states will have to take rigorous action. The refusal of even just a few, let alone many, states to move swiftly could lead to huge costs for humanity as a whole. COVID-19 concentrates this challenge. Whereas climate change represents a long-term drift towards severe ecological distress, dealing with a pandemic takes place on a much shorter timescale, requiring an immediate state response. The crisis also underscores the position of the nation-state as the decisive institution of the modern world to deal with these issues. Citizens hold the organic premise that the state should protect their wellbeing with governments accordingly judged against their record in doing so.

The test that COVID-19 has presented to states shows the importance of output legitimacy in the relationship between state and citizens. This refers to a type of authority garnered not through the process of making decisions (which may lack legitimacy) but the substantive outcomes for human wellbeing. As global crises mount, states will be judged against their ability to protect citizens. Authoritarian systems that lack input legitimacy (the process of making decisions) can make up for this in the eyes of citizens through delivering substantive public goods. Vietnam is a compelling example of a form of authoritarian rulership that is responsive to this demand for effective outputs. Heterodox measurements of human wellbeing illustrate the strength of this form of authoritarian protectionism. The Happy Planet Index, for example, uses four elements: citizen satisfaction, life expectancy, inequality of outcomes and ecological footprint. Whereas Vietnam is in the mid-table of the Human Development Index, it rockets to fifth place in the Happy Planet Index, leapfrogging Western states that are traditionally seen as highly advanced (Happy Planet Index, 2016). Although its very high score is largely due to its small ecological footprint (which itself is changing with higher growth), in terms of public health (46 out of 140 analysed states) Vietnam still outperforms many wealthier states (Happy Planet Index, 2016).

Vietnam is not the only country to have effectively tackled COVID-19, but it is a striking example of how economic wealth is not the decisive determinant of success. Its case should be taken as a warning of the potential legitimacy boost authoritarian states can receive in a crisis. Nonetheless, this is also not the general pattern. There has been no one model of response from the world's authoritarian states to the pandemic. Instead we see radically different policies and postures.

Government via chaos? Different forms of authoritarian protectionism in the COVID-19 crisis

Pathogens may mutate into different forms through their lifecycle but their transmission through the world's polities involves a relatively straightforward modular replication from one human carrier to the next. Metaphorical contagions of the authoritarian variety are, by contrast, radically more pluralistic.

Indeed, there has not been a single model of authoritarian response to COVID-19 (Renton, 2020). The diverse reactions of the authoritarian protectionists illustrate how despite the commonalities in their orientation they still diverge in profound ways over how they conceptualize public authority. This has had a decisive impact on how they pursued their health policy response.

The regimes of Nguyễn Phú Trọng in Vietnam and Xi Jinping in China stand at one end of the spectrum. This approach uses the capacity of the one-party state to undertake central coordination in order to prioritize public health. The strict lockdowns pursued in these states, in turn, have a knock-on effect for the economy, allowing the lifting of restrictions faster following the isolation of the disease. This 'zero COVID' strategy seeks to reduce the spread of the virus to a very low level. Once cases subsequently arise, they are then small in number and can be dealt with through systematic testing combined with case isolation and contact-tracing among the infected. The ability to pursue a 'zero COVID' strategy is certainly not the preserve of one-party states. New Zealand, Taiwan and South Korea have all approached the crisis in an analogous way with comparable results. In Vietnam, the negative dimensions of the political model can also be observed through the course of the crisis. The BBC euphemistically described living conditions in its mandatory quarantine facilities, for example, as 'not always luxurious' (A. Jones, 2020), despite their evident rigour in isolating infected citizens from the broader population. As its crisis management boosts the prestige and authority of the state in society, the regime has also taken the opportunity to crack down on dissent with Human Rights Watch reporting numerous arrests for 'political crimes' (Human Rights Watch, 2020). China's lurch towards extreme despotism is all the more severe – and a subject we discuss in the next chapter.

Nonetheless, the unusual institutional forms of the Vietnamese and Chinese systems represent a distinct variety of authoritarian protectionism that emerges with greater global credibility. While no states will seek to replicate the specificities of their internal regime, which reflect arcane legacies of the 20th century, their efficiency will surely have a knock-on ideological effect globally. For the success of one-party systems can only weaken efforts to strengthen the rule-based, multi-party ones.

At the other extreme, yet equally corrosive to the future of democratic governance, lie Trump and Bolsonaro. Both leaders have floundered in the face of the crisis and their particular variety of authoritarianism shares many traits. It exudes market egoism, with opposition to placing restrictions on economic activity to protect public health, and a masculinized dismissal of the dangers the virus represents to themselves, never mind their own citizens. Bolsonaro has repeatedly called public health efforts by his own government into question. On 11 March 2020, that is, a week and a half after the publication of the WHO-China report, Bolsonaro claimed, in direct contradiction to the WHO's warning to the world, 'there are other kinds of flu which have killed more people than that one' (Robertson, 2020). At the end of March, he referred to governors creating quarantine lockdowns as 'job killers', and said of the pandemic, 'some people will die, they will die, that's life' (Robertson, 2020). In April, he openly flouted guidelines on social distancing, attending a demonstration of supporters to oppose lockdown quarantine measures, which saw some participants hold placards calling for a military coup and the shutting down of the Supreme Court (*BBC News*, 2020d). Bolsonaro then sacked his own health advisor for disagreeing with his opposition to physical distancing (Robertson, 2020). The effect of these failings was as predictable as it was tragic. By 9 September 2020 over four million Brazilians had tested positive for the virus and 127,000 had lost their lives (Johns Hopkins University Coronavirus Resource Centre, 2020).

Trump adopted the same posture to the pandemic and the risks it presented. Disdainful of public health advice, he asserted a similarly macho disregard for his own safety and made keeping the economy open the absolute priority during the critical month following the WHO report. On 21 March 2020, three weeks after the WHO analysis, Trump ruled out a nationwide lockdown (Hoyle and Spencer, 2020). Like in Brazil, state governors acted regardless, with 158 million Americans in lockdown conditions two days later (*New York Times*, 2020a). Even then Trump claimed that the lockdown would be over by Easter, promising 'packed churches' at a 'beautiful time' to re-open the country (Bennett, 2020).

Perhaps unsurprisingly given their complete disregard for the public health risks that COVID-19 posed, both Bolsonaro and Trump became infected with the illness. They used their experience to shrug off the virus and project an image of masculine invincibility in the face of danger. On his return to the White House, Trump released a video on his Twitter account steeped in militarized, 'strongman' political nationalism, concluding with him symbolically ripping off his mask on the White House steps (Trump, 2020d). On the same day, in a tweet that Twitter judged to violate its new rules on misinformation, he joined Bolsonaro in comparing COVID-19 to seasonal flu. 'In most populations', he claimed, erroneously, COVID-19 is 'far less lethal' (Trump, 2020e). Five days later, in another tweet judged to break the company's misinformation rules, he said, 'A total and complete sign off from White House Doctors yesterday. That means I can't get it (immune), and can't give it' (Trump, 2020f). These statements are overflowing with a masculinized image of a strongman emerging triumphant from battle.

To understand this appeal and how masculinity is instrumentalized we might consider Michael Kimmel's argument regarding patriarchy, which states that it is 'not simply [a register of] men's power over women; it's also some men's power over other men' (Kimmel and Wade, 2018, p 237; see also Kimmel, 2013). He argues the terms associated with masculinity in the words of men themselves demonstrate that it constitutes a coded set of behaviours that seek validation from, and power over, other men. Kimmel recalls asking a group of American soldiers to define what they considered masculine behaviour to be. They replied by saying, '[t]ough, strong, never show weakness, win at all costs, suck it up, play through pain, be competitive, get rich, get laid' (Kimmel and Wade, 2018, p 238). In this rendition a performative opposition to a sense of one's own frailty or vulnerability becomes a means of projecting power over other, supposedly weaker, men. In the American and Brazilian cases this also connects easily with elements of cultural memory, for 'the roots of such selfish, anti-empathetic, armed masculinity run deep' (Harsin, 2020, p 1065) in each national tradition. Notably, for our purposes, in asserting this masculine egoism, Trump and Bolsonaro do not appear, at least at first sight, to advance a claim of protection, as such. Their 'strongman' leadership offers instead a survival of the fittest maxim.

Recall, however, that authoritarian protectionism starts with the simple maxim: 'the world may end for other and not for us', that is, its concept of protection is always selective, burdened by ethnic identity and masculinized in potentially divergent ways. Gendered notions of national identity can take a variety of forms, switching between masculine and other conceptions of male leadership. Indeed, when Kimmel asked the same group of soldiers whether masculine behaviour was the same as 'good' male behaviour they responded by saying it was not. Instead they associated good male behaviour with other characteristics: 'Honor, duty, integrity, sacrifice, do the right thing, stand up for the little guy, be a provider, *be a protector*' (Kimmel and Wade, 2018, p 238, emphasis added). When asked where they got these ideas from, they said: 'Well, it's everywhere. It's our culture, it's Homeric, it's Shakespearean, it's the Judeo-Christian heritage' (Kimmel and Wade, 2018, p 238). While such characteristics of integrity, sacrifice and so on could easily be seen as universal values, for this group of men, they were *gendered* and *culturally specific* to the West.

So, whether they approach a situation as a protector (the good male) or egotistical aggressor (masculine male) the choice is constrained by a common register of gendered ideas about cultural belonging. The same person may choose protective or masculine postures at different times and the co-existence of these images within their idea of maleness frames the choice.

We can say something similar about Trump and Bolsonaro. Their brand of authoritarian protectionism moves between different images: it combines a performative, masculine egoism with a conception of the 'good man' that does indeed claim to protect their respective nations from threats. The structures of family, nation and religion allow these different images, the male aggressor and protector, to become integrated and normalized as two sides of the same appeal for strong leadership. To link these elements Trump and Bolsonaro both draw on a militarized discourse – a move which has a faultless logic at the level of symbolism. What, after all, combines more clearly the ideological registers of aggression and protection than the totem of the armed forces? Trump calls his grassroots electoral campaign 'army for Trump', seeking supporters to 'enlist' to 'fight' the 'Radical Democrats and Fake News Media' (Trump, 2020g). Posting this to social media he called on supporters to 'Volunteer to be a Trump Election Poll Watcher', with a large image saying 'fight for President Trump' (Trump, 2020h), an oblique reference to his call for White militias to 'stand by' and 'monitor' the vote.

In both these guises – the protective and the aggressive – the point of consistency lies in the concept of the people being embroiled in a state of war against enemies within and without. Trump promises to defeat the 'China virus' and 'Make America Great Again'. Bolsonaro declares 'Brazil Above Everything, God Above Everyone'. Both accuse their opponents of corruption, of abandoning Christian values, of peddling fake news and promoting socialism and communism. The political field is thus poisoned as an alleged life and death struggle to save the nation from deadly threats is pursued.

The crux of the opportunity for authoritarianism

Are we – as Brexit Party leader Nigel Farage said at the outset of the crisis – 'all nationalists now'? (Farage, 2020). Farage was quick to identify the crisis as an opportunity for his brand of radical right politics. The triumph of this mindset of authoritarian protectionism in the face of the crisis is not inevitable (for a cautionary note, see Bieber, 2020), but the pandemic provides 'raw material', so to speak, that can be welded to the ideological priorities of the nationalist right. In how it is cognitively apprehended and imagined by global populations outside of China, the crisis is filtered into the minds of the public as a mortal threat that comes from 'somewhere else', that is, the outside world. And while this conception of the crisis as an international condition – a feature of the world's sociological makeup as a plurality of interconnected societies – can be drawn on to catalyse a politics of global cooperation, this requires a much more active, politically conscious intervention. For the 'default option', the spontaneous element of populations and their leaders is to seek *national protection* from the virus.

This was evident in the wave of border closures occurring across Europe at the outset of the pandemic. And while these temporary restrictions on the movement of people are just that – time-limited in their character – they might demonstrate how nationalistic responses can be visceral. By contrast, the internationalist alternative has to fight this common sense. Even events exhibiting logics hostile to authoritarian protectionism underline the default character of nationalism. Consider the steps to reform the Eurozone, for example, which have been rightly heralded as a major step forward for international cooperation. The negotiations that delivered the reform were subject to such intense horse trading between states that they inadvertently reaffirmed the central role of national conflict in Europe.

The xenophobic treatment of the virus as a foreign threat welds the crisis to the assumptions of ethnic nationalism. From an early stage Trump labelled COVID-19 as the 'Chinese virus' or 'China virus'.

Hindu nationalists in India have also engaged in the 'politics of naming' (Lindaman and Viala-Gaudefroy, 2020), linking the virus to their favoured forms of racism and xenophobia with 'Coronajihad' becoming a widely circulated term among the general public (Gopal, 2020). Scapegoating minorities plays a performative role in the power play of authoritarian protectionism. It allows leaders to mobilize the language of protection against phantom threats. For those in power this has the added benefit of deflection: the blame for the unfolding chaos always lies at the door of 'others'.

Long crises in world history – these extended paroxysms of reordering and breakdown – provide a series of opportunities for anti-democratic politics. The new authoritarian protectionists act as the ultimate multiplier effect in the long crisis of the 21st century. They arise as a result of combined breakdowns found in the human ecology, economic conditions and international relations, and amplify further these tendencies. We seem today to be living through such a spiral effect.

FIVE

Sino-America

You know what I am? I'm a nationalist.
Donald Trump, speaking at a campaign
rally in October 2018

The Chinese people have been indomitable and persistent,
we have the spirit of fighting the bloody battle against our
enemies to the bitter end.
Xi Jinping, speech to the National
People's Congress, 2018

The polity of Hong Kong has a special place in underlining
the geopolitical inflections of the new authoritarian protectionism. Hong Kong's youthful, militant democratic movement
found support from the most hardline parts of the new, radical
right Republican Party. Ted Cruz, a figure from the party's
ultra-conservative wing, whose second place to Trump in
the 2016 primary contest underlined just how far the party
had moved to the right, has even been subject to targeted
sanctions from the Chinese government due to his role in
pushing a combative line on human rights abuses in Congress.
Yet, his support for the democratic process did not extend to
the domestic politics of the United States. When Congress
was hastily reconvened after the mob insurrection, to precede
with certifying the result, Cruz maintained his opposition. He

continued to back Trump's malicious attack on the peaceful transfer of power. It seemed Hong Kongers had his support because they were fighting China and communism, rather than out of a general commitment to the institutions of liberal and democratic government.

Hong Kong pushed itself into the centre of Sino-American relations due to the extraordinary scale of its struggle for democratic rights over the last decade. This has represented the most serious challenge to communist rule since the Tiananmen Square protests of 1989. Hong Kongers stepped up their fight for democracy at a moment when the Chinese state was moving in the opposite direction: towards a much more centralized and authoritarian system. Xi Jinping assumed the position of party General Secretary in November 2012, becoming Chinese president in March the following year. Today he has become the most powerful Chinese leader since Deng Xiaoping. His reforms, which began with an anti-corruption drive, over time morphed into the creation of a highly personalized dictatorship.

Xi's rule has dramatically altered the relationship between Hong Kong and the Chinese mainland. In less than a decade a number of students, academics and civil society activists have gone from the fringes to the centre of Hong Kong's public debate. Many are now household names, known for their defiant stance against China's authoritarian turn. Benny Tai, the legal academic and democracy activist, argued in 2014 that what then seemed like a gradual deterioration of the rule of law necessitated a new push for political reform. He was engaged in a high-profile campaign for universal suffrage which would contribute to the 'Umbrella Movement' protests of autumn 2014, the prelude to the even larger and more militant uprising of 2019–2020. "We have already got a rule of law, but how to maintain it? We need to have a democratic system to sustain it", he observed (interview with Benny Tai, August 2014). Just under six years later, Tai was sacked from his academic position at Hong Kong University. While nominally for a criminal conviction he received for his role in peaceful protests, it was widely seen as a purely political move, reflecting the demands of the pro-Beijing executive in Hong Kong. His own personal experience tragically confirmed the veracity of his prediction on the rule of law.

Tai is part of the older generation of Hong Kong democrats. The new younger movement would become associated with figures like Alex Chow, formerly the General Secretary of the Hong Kong Student Federation, Nathan Law, Tiffany Yuen and Joshua Wong. Chow argued at the outset that the movement went beyond a fight for liberal values. It formed part of broader struggle for social justice. "We call for democracy because we need to have choice, we have to have autonomy, we have to have the things behind democracy, a more equalized society, a more just society", he explains (interview with Alex Chow, August 2014). This younger generation would dominate the wave of protests. They were often bolder in their demands. Like Tai, Chow also experienced the rapid deterioration in political freedom in Hong Kong across these years. In 2017, he was given, along with two other prominent young activists, a seven-month prison sentence in charges related to the 2014 protests. The Chinese regime was laying down a clear marker with its preparedness to create a new generation of political prisoners.

The activity and energy of the new, young democracy movement, coupled with frustration and anger over Chinese authoritarianism in the polity, created a new dynamic in Hong Kong public opinion. Five years ago, it was common for democracy activists to argue that if a free vote on the basis of universal suffrage was permitted for the office of Chief Executive, a pro-Beijing candidate would still win. Tai observed back in 2014, for instance, that the majority of Hong Kongers did not back civil disobedience and that this underlined the extent of support Beijing could expect in free elections:

'If … [they] can assemble some 1 million people signing a statement supporting their demands, that means they have a very big social base. Why worry about a demo-cratic election? They will be able to win. We also make the point that in no case will the Hong Kong people vote for a pan-Democratic person to be chief executive, as they know such a person cannot work with Beijing … The Communist Party know that in 2017 a pro-Beijing candidate will be elected … but they want 100 per cent control.' (Interview with Benny Tai, 20 August 2014)

One-hundred per cent control could be a compelling sum-mary of Xi Jinping's rulership since 2012. Tai's caution on the strength of anti-Beijing feeling reflected the mood of many Hong Kong democrats at the time. But in the period since the situation changed dramatically. The 2019 local government elections, taking place in the context of huge pro-democratic protests, were largely seen as a referendum on them. Turnout leapt to 71 per cent and pro-democratic forces won a land-slide victory. The result was an emphatic demonstration of popular hostility to the Beijing government. Both the level of participation and outcome were unprecedented in Hong Kong's history. The extraordinary scale of unrest seen in the 2019–2020 protests lay behind the shock. During this period Hong Kong had not only seen mass demonstrations but a gen-eral strike, the storming of the Legislative Council building, and huge occupations of university campuses put under 'siege' by security forces. The level of violent repression the movement experienced and scale of popular resistance had no precedent in Hong Kong history.

While not unconnected to the earlier protests for universal suffrage, the uprising of 2019 was defensive. Plans for a national security law that would provide the authorities with blanket powers to deal with 'subversion against the central government' caused public outrage. They were rightly seen as amounting to the de facto end of Hong Kong's special status and polit-ical freedoms. Hong Kongers who had been prepared to give Beijing the benefit of the doubt switched as the end of the polity's precious freedoms and special status came into view. Under pressure the national security law was withdrawn by the Hong Kong government, only to be imposed unilaterally by Beijing in June 2020.

The movement was defeated and the space for political dissent significantly narrowed. As the authorities launch a string of mass arrests many activists are now fleeing the polity. Hong Kong became trapped in the authoritarian net of Sino-America. The city-state was unable to reconcile its citizens' demands for democracy with the authoritarian turn in Beijing, and soon found itself on the cultural, economic and geopolitical frontline of the breakdown in US–China relations.

Trump and Xi: the distorted mirror image

At its apex the long crisis of the 21st century can be read as a conflict (and negotiation) over the management of economic and ecological risk by the two pre-eminent world powers: China and the United States. Globalization turned these states into lucrative trading partners. US corporations benefited from the outsourcing revolution, taking advantage of cheap labour they helped drive forward the process of Chinese industrialization. China, in turn, converted many of the dollars it earnt through its large trade surplus with America into funding US public debt, until June 2019 it was the biggest global lender to the federal government (Amadeo, 2020). For those benefiting from the globalization paradigm this was a win-win situation all round. Yet, under Trump and Xi, Sino-American relations hit rock bottom. Although Trump's stop–start trade war with China has not shifted the fundamentals of their economic relationship, the language his government uses carries strong echoes of the Reaganite rhetoric towards the Soviet Union in the early 1980s, declaring that America 'has finally awoken to the threat the Chinese Communist Party's actions … pose to our very way of life' (O'Brien, 2020). In some respects, this new conflict could be seen as a phenomenon found repeatedly across history: the 'rise and fall' of great powers, whose dominance is eventually superseded by stronger or more nimble competitors (Kennedy, 1989). But this is insufficient to capture the complexity of the Sino-American interrelationship, and particularly the forces that led to the new politics of Trump and Xi.

American power after 1989 certainly enjoyed a near complete international dominance over the globalizing world system. The US was militarily unmatchable once the Soviet Union collapsed; geopolitically, the country enjoyed extraordinary diplomatic influence; and economically it shaped the new world order, as trade and financialization allowed American capital to globalize helped by the security of the global dollar system (Gowan, 1999). One illustration of the dominance the US (and its like-minded British ally) enjoyed is Foreign Direct Investment (FDI) flows. The *1997 World Investment Report* noted how FDI had hit a new record, $350 billion, and that this was 'driven primarily by investments originating in just two countries – the United States and the United Kingdom' (UNCTAD, 1997, p xvi). These two states made up nearly half (47 per cent) of all FDI flows going to developing countries, reflecting the strength of Wall Street and the City of London in the new, thoroughly neoliberal, economic order. Yet, this Anglo-American dominance was not without challengers. And the difference between the Reaganite conflict with the Soviet Union in the 1980s lies in the deep economic relationship that the United States has built with China over the last three decades. Unlike the autarchic and statist Soviet system, China has become a crucial nodal point in the combined structure of global capitalism.

China played the globalization game skilfully. It opened up sufficiently to benefit from international capital invest-ment and export opportunities, but was also geopolitically strong enough to negotiate favourable terms of engagement with the US-led world. The story of this success can also be read in terms of the metric of FDI. In 1997, while China had established itself as a major recipient country for FDI, its overseas investments were negligible (UNCTAD, 1997, p 5). But just over two decades later this has changed completely. China is today a major source of capital for the rest of the world. The *2019 World Investment Report* observes this marked turnaround, 'the United States and China – in joint first place – [are] the most likely sources of foreign investment' (UNCTAD, 2019, p 16). Not only is China now the world's largest economy once adjusted for purchasing power parity, but it has achieved this position through a model of development quite different to the prevalent one in the West (McFarlane, 2020). It combines highly centralized state coordination with free market capitalism, an unusual amalgam that has proven especially effective.

Yet, in its political qualities, China sometimes appears as a distorted mirror image of Trump's America. In October 2019, as violent conflict continued to rage between the Hong Kong authorities and the democratic protest movement, Xi Jinping issued a stark warning. 'Anyone who attempts to split any region from China will perish, with their bodies smashed and bones ground to powder', he said (*BBC News*, 2019). This mobilization of violent imagery in the service of political nationalism has some resonance with the language that Trump used in response to the Black Lives Matter mass protests a year later. Trump denounced protestors as 'professional anarchists' and 'violent mobs', committing acts of 'domestic' terror, declaring his intention to protect America from this enemy within. As police clashed with protestors across America, Trump cast himself as the people's last saviour. 'I am your president of law and order', he said (Trump, 2020i). At St. John's Episcopal Church, opposite the White House, he posed for photos clutching a bible, and promised to make a 'great country … even greater' (C-Span, 2020). This piece of blatant political theatre inevitably drew the, possibly intentional, comparison with the often-repeated warning that 'when fascism comes to America it will be wrapped in the flag and carrying a cross'. As

Trump called on the military to 'dominate the streets' (Trump, 2020i), America appeared at a civilizational nadir; US democracy was facing its most serious crisis in the post-war era.

Trump and Xi, despite heading radically different political systems, draw from a comparable pool of ideological images, which, above all, appear to value violence as a tool to enforce unity. Both pursue authoritarian protectionism, but in distinct forms, sharing a vision of a strong state aggressively prosecuting the interests of the national people, against their alleged enemies within and without.

To read the current conjuncture historically requires considering how distinct development paths combined to elicit the turn to authoritarian protectionism on either side of the Sino-American divide (on this see Harvey, 2007). In China, a 'late', but extremely concentrated and rapid process of industrialization transformed the cost base of world production with a large injection of cheap labour. It turned the country into a major world power and, despite its capitalist logic, was carried through by a 'communist' state. This trajectory in China was combined globally with the neoliberal shift towards a financialized economy in the West where inflation in asset prices offered high rewards to capital, but with investment in the real economy and productivity stagnant wage levels remained depressed (Piketty, 2014; Stiglitz, 2019). While this generated high inequality in the Western world the explosive political backlash it elicited does not fit neatly onto a rich/poor divide.

Hillary Clinton had a significant lead among low income voters, 53 per cent of those earning less than US$30,000 a year and 52 per cent in the US$30,000–49,999 band (CNN, 2016) – a fact that is often recounted to undermine the claim the Trump phenomena constituted a 'working class revolt'. However, this was a significant fall from previous elections – between 2000 and 2012 the Democrats won, on average, 61.2 per cent of the low income vote (Stonecash, 2017, p 39). Trump made inroads into the White component of the working class, which built on gains the Republicans had already made in 2008. Consequently, in 2016 Clinton's support among White voters 'with a high school degree or less and those in the lower third of the income distribution is the lowest level recorded [by a Democratic canditate] since 1952' (Stonecash, 2017, p 36).[1] Trump's authoritarian protectionism helped the Republicans to build a broader electoral coalition in class terms, supplementing their traditional support among affluent and high income voters with an influx of blue-collar support. So, this was not a 'working class revolt' but a cross-class hegemonic movement united around a deeply reactionary, ethnic nationalist political agenda.

The geography of this transformation played a key role. Big cities, like London and New York, where huge wealth exists side by side with biting poverty did not lead the authoritarian protectionist revolt. Instead the small towns and depressed rural areas, struggling to carve out a position in the new economy, generated the political shock with counties that voted Clinton accounting for some two thirds of American GDP (Muro and Liu, 2016). The long shadow of Chinese industrialization stood over these developments. Regions that had experienced deindustrialization as a result of Chinese import competition rallied to the cause of 'America first' (Colantone and Stanig, 2018; Rosenberg and Boyle, 2019). These 'geographies of discontent' have proven fertile ground for right-wing populism across Europe, too (Dijkstra et al, 2020). Notably, it is the 'left behind' town, geography, and not social class, that has driven these explosions. In these places, it is often the relatively affluent, the home-owning middle strata, not necessarily directly impacted by deindustrialization but experiencing the knock-on cultural effects of boarded up shops and run-down high streets, that turned to the new authoritarianism (Antonucci et al, 2017; Rodríguez-Pose, 2018; Jennings and Stoker, 2019).

So, the industrial rise of China was a factor in creating the geographies of discontent that were an important dimension of the Trump victory. But contrary to the claims of his administration, which, for political reasons, argues American deindustrialization only began in the late 1990s, and particularly with the entry of China into the World Trade Organization in 2001, the process of decline goes back to the Reagan era. Deregulation, low investment and the shift from the real economy to finance went alongside competitive pressure from Japan to hit US manufacturing jobs (Lopez, 2017). The Clinton and Bush Jr administrations maintained this model, while competition from China added to the jobs crisis. Since 1997, the United States has lost 91,000 manufacturing plants and millions of factory jobs. But most of these losses occurred in particular spikes: 'the 2001 recession and the China import surge of 2002–2004, and during the Great Recession of 2008–2009—account for more than all of the net loss of nearly 5 million manufacturing jobs in this period' (Scott, 2020). Trump saw an opportunity in these conditions.

The aftermath of the 2008 financial crisis is of special significance here as both a political and economic moment. Economically it underlined the exhaustion of neoliberal globalization, tipping the world into prolonged period of crisis, but the political rupture was perhaps all the more extraordinary. The fallout from the crisis created a deep sense of despair and anxiety that ethnic nationalism exploited.

Coming from a Republican candidate some of Trump's interventions were rather remarkable. In Pennsylvania, June 2016, a state Trump went on to win by a mere 44,000 votes, he gave a stump speech that was positively 'leftish' in its discourses, even 'confessing' his own status as a member of the elite:

> Our politicians have aggressively pursued a policy of globalization, moving our jobs, our wealth and our factories to Mexico and overseas. Globalization has made the financial elite, who donate to politicians, very, very wealthy. I used to be one of them. I hate to say it, but I used to be one. But it has left millions of our workers

with nothing but poverty and heartache. When subsidized foreign steel is dumped into our markets, threatening our factories, the politicians have proven, folks, have proven they do nothing. (Trump, 2016)

The language was very similar to Bernie Sanders' – who was also name-checked positively in the speech. To acknowledge this aspect is not to detract from Trump's racism. In his 2016 campaign he called for a ban on Muslims entering the United States, referred to Mexican immigrants as rapists and made a string of other shocking statements (for a catalogue of Trump's racist remarks, see Lopez, 2016). But we do need to recognize how Trump connected this rabid nationalism to a critique of globalization and economic injustice. The combination of these elements distilled his vision of authoritarian protectionism, cultivating Trump's image as a champion of a blue-collar America at the mercy of globalist elites. The power of this appeal can be seen very clearly in the result. Of the top 25 states by manufacturing workforce Trump won some 80 per cent of the electoral college 'votes'[2] (Scott, 2020).

'The Chinese Dream': on the Xi model of authoritarian protectionism

China's shift to the aggressive posture of authoritarian protectionism similarly constitutes a mid-range effect of the 2008 economic crisis. But from a different historical perspective: a rising hegemon with confidence, in a decaying American-led world. Chinese elites and commentators recognized this as a turning point in global power, a crisis moment for American leadership on the international stage. As Elizabeth Economy argues, Xi should be seen as part of a group of Chinese officials who 'believed that the financial crisis represented [such] an inflection point in world history', above all characterized by 'the decline of the United States and the rise of China' (Economy, 2018, p 188). It requires, this group argues, a new

Chinese assertiveness that translates the country's industrial power into global influence.

In the Chinese case, authoritarian protectionism might seem an inappropriate register of analysis to use in non-democratic societies; for it assumes the exercise of power within the polity requires legitimization. But whether a ruler or party is democratically elected or not, is a separate issue to how they justify their rule. All leaders, regardless of the formal institutional setting, seek legitimacy with the use of ideas, values and policies. These will tend to involve claims about identity and belonging, which create the sense that rulers and ruled share common interests. Indeed, dictatorial regimes, from the fascist to softer autocracies, have throughout history been highly ideological and derived legitimacy from their aggressive prosecution of the alleged interests of particular groups in society. And there are clear elements of authoritarian protectionism in the more outwardly ideological posture China has assumed under Xi. His brand of nationalism involves the use of an ethnically homogenous conception of the people, and aggressively asserts the primacy of their partisan interests against dissident minorities.

Nonetheless, it should also be acknowledged that on the surface level of ideological statements, Xi stands firmly within the ideological tradition of his predecessors. Indeed, considering adherence to 'Xi Jinping Thought' has been written into the Chinese constitution, the body of ideas it draws together are strikingly unoriginal. His three-volume work, *The Governance of China*, could arguably have been written at any point in the era of Deng Xiaoping and after. It compiles various speeches and writings of Xi and has been translated into a number of languages, perhaps reflecting the Chinese Communist Party (CCP)'s new global 'turn'.

Xi gives particular emphasis to 'the Chinese Dream', which he defines as the 'rejuvenation of the Chinese nation' that 'embodies the long-cherished hope of several generations of the Chinese people, gives expression to the overall interests of the Chinese nation and the Chinese people, and represents the shared aspiration of all the sons and daughters of the Chinese nation' (Xi, 2015, np). As this implies, the Chinese president stands firmly within the long tradition of Chinese communism that has since its inception made extensive use of political nationalism as a critical source of popular legitimacy. His choice of ideological language is, in formal terms, very similar to previous Chinese leaders that spoke of the 'invigoration of China' (Deng), the 'great rejuvenation of the Chinese nation' (Jiang Zemin) and the 'harmonious society' (Hu Jintao) (see Wang, 2013). Crucially, Xi declares in favour of 'socialism with Chinese characteristics', the summary description used by Deng to justify the capitalist turn to pro-market reform. Nonetheless, insofar as there is a shift in vocabulary, it is towards the idea of a *China that protects*; one that offers all Chinese wellbeing and security. As Zheng Wang explains:

> Instead of only emphasizing the Chinese Dream as the goal for the country and the government, Xi endeavoured to convince the general public that the dream was also for each individual Chinese. And the realization of this dream for the country would be the catalyst for the realization of the dream for the individual, including housing, employment, public health, education and environment. Thus, the Chinese public could feel connected with the Chinese Dream narrative. (Wang, 2013)

Under Xi, however, we also find a shift in how the Chinese people are ethnically imagined towards a more homogenous conception of the national community (what we have called in this book, the first logic of authoritarian protectionism). Xi's emphasis on the inclusive Chinese dream as protective has gone alongside a more overtly assimilationist concept of the national ethnic community (which means, in the Chinese setting, the Han-Chinese as the largest ethnic group). Hints at this are contained in *The Governance of China* but in terms that are broadly consistent with the longer tradition of Chinese nationalism. Xi argues that 'to realize the Chinese Dream, we must foster ... the national spirit with patriotism at its core' (Xi, 2015, np). Furthermore, this is held to be a requirement of 'all ethnic groups' that 'must foster the great national spirit and follow the call of the times, strengthen our inner bond of unity and perseverance, and vigorously march towards the future' (Xi, 2015, np). Perhaps more significantly, this was given particular emphasis at the 19th Party Congress in 2017, the landmark moment for Xi's authority as his 'Thought' was written into the party constitution. The conference established a more 'integrationist' approach based on 'consolidating an integrated consciousness of the Chinese nation' and 'interethnic contact, exchange and mingling' (Zhao and Leibold, 2020, p 499).

In short, at the level of official state ideology, we can uncover two clear elements of authoritarian protectionism: a definition of the Chinese people implicitly defined in an ethnically homogenous way *and* a socially inclusive claim to the protection of this group as part of a common 'dream'. We do not need, however, to merely read between the lines of the secular ideology that Chinese communism represents; for Xi's political practice has involved a clear ethnic nationalist element.

Tai – the scholar-activist whose sacking we discussed at the outset of the chapter – was singled out for persecution in Hong Kong not simply because of his civil society activity seeking universal suffrage, but also due to his scholarly work, which advanced a legal argument that the people of the city-state region had a right to self-determination. In 2018, at an academic seminar in Taiwan, Tai argued that in a situation of democratic change on Mainland China, the various local/ national groups, such as the Hong Kongers, Shanghainese and Uyghurs, would have a right to discuss their self-determination, including independence, autonomy or creating a hybrid structure like the EU (Wong, 2018). This was consistent with his earlier remarks and did not amount to an unqualified call for independence. But it was condemned in a wave of hostility from the pro-Beijing establishment, including a rare official statement from the Hong Kong government (Cheng, 2018). In the background to this attack is the 'localist turn' in Hong Kong, which has seen a vocal and committed minority advocate independence from Beijing, a sentiment especially strong among the younger generation of activists (on this see Lam and Cooper, 2017). Localists contest the core claim of Chinese sovereignty in Hong Kong and elicit a furious reaction from the CCP for doing so. Beijing recognizes this movement has implications for its internal political unity and external territorial claims in the region, notably over Taiwan. Indeed, the case of Hong Kong simply gives a pronounced illustration of the tensions over ethnic and local identities, belonging, language rights and their associated political claims in Chinese sovereign territory. Efforts undertaken to impose greater integration, in a political space where a predominantly Han-Chinese party retains an unchallengeable monopoly on power, make such communal issues inevitable.

In Xinjiang, the persecution of the Uyghur people, the Turkic-speaking, Muslim minority, has given an all the more extreme illustration of Xi's authoritarian protectionist regime. In 2017, the Chinese government established 're-education camps' in the province, as part of its 'people's war on terror' against Muslim separatists. The 1.5 million detainees have faced brutal and chilling conditions which Human Rights Watch describes as a system of 'mass arbitrary detention, torture, forced political indoctrination, and mass surveillance' of the Muslim population (Wang, 2020). Through this brutal means the authorities seek the submission of the Uyghur community to the dictates of Xi Jinping Thought and ruling party ideology more broadly. China traditionally recognizes the Uyghurs as an ethnic minority within 'the unitary multi-ethnic Chinese nation' (The Information Office of the State Council, 2003), and has not formally changed this under Xi. But the reported conditions in the re-education camps amount to a form of 'forced assimilation or destruction of their culture', which is in breach of Article 8 of the United Nations Declaration on the Rights of Indigenous Peoples (United Nations General Assembly, 2007). The Uyghur community have also been used as forced labour and – perhaps unsurprisingly given China's economic clout – their products circulate in global trade. A 2020 report found forced labour had entered 'the supply chains of at least 82 well-known global brands in the technology, clothing and automotive sectors, including Apple, BMW, Gap, Huawei, Nike, Samsung, Sony and Volkswagen' (Xiuzhong Xu et al, 2020). The drive to subordinate this community to the identity of a unitary China has thus gone alongside the creation of a labour market underclass, providing the human material for big corporate names in the 'liberal' West. This seems to speak to the way in which contemporary authoritarianism is adapting organically to the demands of global capitalism, rather than at odds with it.

The denial of free cultural expression by state institutions, which are predominantly Han-Chinese and advance a unitary national identity, means that Xi's China has imposed an ethnically homogenous conception of the people, in all but name. Whereas in 2003 China recognized the religious freedom of the Uyghurs (The Information Office of the State Council, 2003), in the new, less tolerant atmosphere under Xi, their religion has been described as tantamount to a drug addiction by the authorities, 'sick thinking' to be treated by a 'benevolent state' (cited in Raza, 2019, p 497). Both logics one (ethnic homogenization) and two (partisan interests) of authoritarian protectionism are thus present here: the sane, healthy and loyal Han majority are let down by an ill, disloyal group in need of state discipline. The partisan interests of the – implicitly Han – nation lie in suppressing the minority.

Xi's preference for a form of Han-Chinese nationalism perhaps belies a sense of vulnerability at the prospect of separatist demands. It challenges directly the notion of China as an imperial civilization that forms parts of his 'dream' perspective (for a discussion of China's conception of history, see Mayer,

2018). 'Chinese civilization, with a history going back more than 5,000 years provides strong intellectual support for the country's ceaseless self-improvement and growth', as Xi puts it (Xi, 2015, np). This imperialized territorial nationalism can only tolerate ethnic plurality for as long as it does not seek succession; the moment it does so it represents a grave threat to the interests of the party-state. The turn to Han-Chinese 'integration' simply takes this logic to its ultimate, assimilationist conclusion.

These provide points of commonality and symmetry to the wider landscape of authoritarian protectionism. But there are also differences which reflect the institutional context for Chinese politics. Xi makes repeated references to planning for the long term and the CCP has long argued the merits of its dictatorial system lies in the certainty it brings to development, once freed of the potential 'chaos' of competitive elections. As such, there seems less emphasis on what we have called in this book a temporal emergency – the moments of crisis, the sense of prevailing instability, that authoritarian protectionists use to seize political control and undermine institutions. And although its brand of authoritarianism does promote the 'othering' of minorities (for example, the 'sick thinking' of Islam), it does not require these partisan, ethnic interests to be actively mobilized. The legitimacy it draws from these narratives remains largely passive. Indeed, when ethnic nationalist feelings erupt, such as in the 2012 anti-Japanese riots, the party's approach to these outbursts is cautious, rather than facilitative (Wallace and Weiss, 2015).

The Han-Chinese majority has also been subjected to an extraordinary increase in control and surveillance under the Xi government – on a level that makes China qualitatively more authoritarian, at least in its 'institutional' form, than any of the other cases discussed across this book. Under his rule, the PRC has re-inserted itself into Chinese society in a profound manner – reversing the years of more passive retreat from society in the market-reform era. The party has created controversial (at least globally) 'social credit systems' to collect data on individual citizens, and then ranks them according to their 'trustworthiness'. This Orwellian approach has led to the use of disturbing 'blacklists' of citizens labelled as untrustworthy by the state. China justifies this model as a mere extension of the credit rating agency. The latter also takes an element of everyday life – trust – and commercializes it to make a judgement on an individual's ability to pay back a loan (on this see Davies, 2020, p 12). What makes China's system different and more chilling is its attempt to regulate the social behaviours of citizens, not simply their ability to pay back a loan. Although China aims to create a centralized system, there are currently a myriad of different social credit platforms, run by both state authorities and private companies. But the principle of them is simple: individuals are scored on a range of metrics to determine whether they are good citizens or not. 'Bad' behaviours range from misdemeanours like poor driving, playing loud music or jaywalking, to failing to pay public fines; and good behaviours include charity work and giving blood. Even their defenders accept that 'social credit systems and the credibility associated with the scores have become critical in Chinese society' (Raghunath, 2020, p 4). Their apparent popularity (Kostka, 2019) may lie in the perception they give meritocratic 'scores'. Thus, for the CCP it offers some sense of popular legitimacy without democracy. Most importantly, the opportunities for enforcing control are highly attractive to a one-party state determined to impose its will. Spreading fake news, for example, is a widely cited 'bad behaviour', open to the state's misinterpretation to close down criticism.

Significantly, the Chinese credit systems take two major features of contemporary capitalism (Davies, 2020, pp 9–17), the rise of large digital platforms (Facebook et al) interacting constantly with consumers (with associated privacy risks) and the need for debt and finance, and places the authoritarian state at the centre of these social relations. Similar trends exist in democratic societies but in less developed forms. The Snowden leaks exposed an entire structure of state surveillance that had access to the information universe – full of granular detail on individual citizens' lives – created by the major digital platforms (Zuboff, 2019). But while this data has been used for political purposes (illegally in some cases), the Chinese system is on a quite different level: a new form of digitized authoritarian governance. There are few comparable examples of mining digital data in order to score trust and loyalty, or to provide (as in some versions) opportunities for citizens to score/rank their peers.

The Chinese relationship of private capital to the state is also highly distinct. Few believe that the American state has an overarching power over the digital mega corporations, such as Apple. On the contrary, the opposite is arguably true: America and other liberal states have proven highly vulnerable to 'capture' by major corporate interests. China under Xi has pursued a very different model in which private corporations are expected to serve the interests of the one-party state, which has a deep and 'public' presence in society, embedded firmly in the everyday interactions of ordinary citizens.

Trump versus Xi: competing models of the new authoritarianism

The story of the Sino-American comparison illustrates how a legitimizing narrative that draws from the authoritarian protectionist playbook (ethnic nationalism and partisan interests) can be applied to quite different governing practices. Trump thrives on chaos, as a device that creates the sense of fear and insecurity that he feeds off; the Chinese communist tradition has a deeply held dislike for instability and disruption, seeking at all time control and pacification. Crucially, as noted, their governing practices derive from a different view of the position of the state in relation to the market. China under Xi has closed down the space for private capital to create autonomous spheres beyond the reach of the state. Instead large companies – which, as a rule, have assumed their dominant position in the Chinese market due to generous state support and protection from competition – are expected to publicly support Beijing and accept party interference in their governance. Since the 2008 financial crisis, and even more so through the COVID-19 pandemic, governments in the Western world have also showered corporations with support, primarily through bailout programmes and ultra-loose monetary policy. While in both the Chinese and American varieties, this creates cronyism in the ties between state and market, the power relations in China are quite different. In America, corporations not only retain their full autonomy and freedoms, but have proven adept at capturing the state, that is, are able to mould policy to their preferences. In China, the power relations are reversed: the state is carrying through a 'capture' of private business.

To see how this works in practice, consider the example of China's data giants: Alibaba, the e-commerce company which had a market capitalization of US$581.20 billion as of June 2020; putting it in the top ten global companies by value; Tencent, the online games vendor behind the WeChat social media platform that is ubiquitous in China, which had a market capitalization of US$615 billion as of June 2020, also putting it in the global top ten (Bloomenthal, 2020); and the relatively 'small' Baidu, the Chinese alternative to Google, which is valued at around US$60 billion (Ross, 2020). These companies have risen to dominance through a combination of state aid and protectionism. They are provided with cheap credit, face few regulations restricting their profit making and are protected against foreign competitors, who face barriers to entry in the Chinese market. In return – like all companies operating in China – they have to accept the state surveillance system, underpinned by Xi's wider notion of 'internet sovereignty', that includes a 2016 Cybersecurity Law providing the authorities with sweeping access to internet data (Qiang, 2019). But the 'big three' also grew to a size where they were considered of strategic importance by the state. Consequently, they were made to accept state representatives on the board. The power dynamics at work are shaped by the omnipresent police state that creates an implicit social contract for the ultra-wealthy class: in return for their affluence they are expected to demonstrate at all times their loyalty to Xi or risk losing it all. As China-watcher Derek Scissors of the American Enterprise Institute puts it, the power relations that operate between the Chinese state and private sector are based on the existence of 'real fear, like men with guns fear' (cited in Pandey, 2018).

Beyond the 'big three' data corporates other aspects of China's model are very different to the neoliberal global norms promoted by the West. It has a state-run banking system that uses credit as a means to plan development in the wider economy. And its central bank, the People's Bank of China, controls the flow of capital into and out of the country: a system of 'capital controls' that has been out of fashion in the West since the neoliberal financial reforms of the 1970s and 1980s (McFarlane, 2020). A number of these mechanisms could be usefully practised by democratic states to assert greater control on markets. And this cuts to the heart of the very different – in economic terms – form of authoritarianism prompted in the United States by the Trump administration. In the latter, intervention creates a system of state-supported financialization that socializes the risks of investment while the profits remain privatized. In the COVID-19 pandemic this led to sweeping corporate handouts, which were described by Alexandria Ocasio Cortez on the floor of the House of Representatives as 'one of the largest corporate bailouts with as few strings as possible in American history' (Zeballos-Roig, 2020).

By contrast, 'strings attached' is the very essence of Chinese business policy under Xi. The complexity of this system lies in how it *does* deliver public goods through state management and control of the market (such as its exemplary public health protection in the COVID-19 crisis). But it does so within a political order based on the absolute control of the state under the leadership of Xi. Output legitimacy – as we observed in the last chapter – is pursued to make up for the absence of democracy.

The economics of the authoritarian calculation in the United States and the West

The contemporary far right Republican Party combines – as we discussed in Chapter Two – a hostile posture towards democracy with a mix of hardline market liberalism and an autocratic conservatism steeped with religiosity. The idea of *state* representatives sitting on corporate boards – *à la* China – is anathema to their ideology. This means that when shocks occur, such as they did in 2020, requiring significant state support, the ideology pushes in the direction of bailout capitalism: the state provides support, but gets little in return. This system of state-supported financialization emerged not from design but by default. It is a combination of 'emergency' economic policy in the face of crisis – particularly ultra-low interest rates – and the existing economic model inherited from the 1980s with few controls on the ability of capital to flow across borders. Together this drives up asset prices while blue-collar and middle-income groups' incomes stagnate, creating politically unsustainable levels of economic inequality. As limits on capital movements are considered beyond the realm of the politically acceptable few challenge the status quo. Only bold outriders (Pettifor, 2006, pp 38–84; Stiglitz, 2010) call the Western-led architecture for finance into question. And this economic background has an implication for how authoritarianism is being manifested in the privileged states of the 'rich world'.

Indeed, the incentives driving authoritarianism in the West are very different to those in China. Whereas the latter pursues a form of state-controlled capitalism well suited to its status as a giant 'late developer', and the regime's political desire to assert as much power over market and society as possible, in the West the core authoritarian calculation is different. The far right offer to the elite is simple: nationalism is the best way to maintain support for a capital-centric but state-dependent economic model.

Consider the secretive offshore economy where vast amounts of capital can be hidden from tax collectors and criminal investigators (Glenny, 2017; Bullough, 2018). Changing this would require large economic blocs, such as NAFTA and the EU, to use their power and coordinate international reform. Due to their political nationalism authoritarian protectionists tend to oppose international cooperation along these lines or efforts to move away from the system of light-touch financial regulation more broadly. They are also conservative in relation to economic change. To different degrees they accept the status quo. They actively seek out support for their parties from the very wealthy. This creates a clear potential for an alliance between highly globalist individuals – who enjoy the 'flat Earth' culture created by financial globalization – and the new forces of the radical right. For in a political moment of concern over inequality the new authoritarian protectionists offer a politics that disavowals the core economic structure of blame, targeting instead an assorted range of foreign ills. Even Trump's 'leftist' rhetoric on deindustrialization overwhelming presents it as a problem of Chinese trade and tariff competition, and not the direct policy consequence of the Reaganite turn in US conservatism.

The new radical right Republicanism: the Reaganite alliance with Trump

The Republican Party's shift to the radical right, which sees supporters of Reaganomics aligned with Trump's strongman nationalism, is an extreme example of a working through of this economic logic. Steeped in religiosity many in the party believe they are fighting a millenarian struggle against a social liberalism and multiculturalism that imperils the fundamental values of the Founding Fathers. Voter suppression along with a broader calling into question of democracy finds 'moral' justification in these partisan interests. At a series of behind-closed-doors events during the Republicans' 2020 campaign, which were secretly recorded in a video passed to the *Washington Post*, this mindset was very much in evidence. These events, taking place between February and August, were organized by the Council for National Policy, which, like the Heritage Foundation, is another highly influential network for American conservatives, which was founded in the Reagan period. The events were particularly notable for the frank discussion of voter suppression as a mechanism to push down the Democratic Party vote.

'This is a spiritual battle we are in. This is good versus evil', said Bill Walton, the organization's executive committee president, 'we have to do everything we can to win' (in O'Harrow, 2020). Another Republican activist, Charlie Kirk, was recorded saying it was very welcome that university campuses had been closed due to COVID-19 as less students would vote, 'please keep the campuses closed', he said to loud cheers, 'like it's a great thing' (in O'Harrow, 2020). 'Ballot harvesting' is the name given to the practice of groups completing their mail-in vote together then sending them off in a batch. The contradictory statements that the US right make in relation to it underline how their intense sense of partisan interest cloud any fair assessment of the democratic process. When Trump gave a keynote at the August meeting of the Council for National Policy he condemned this practice – as part of an evidence-free tirade against the alleged fraud being planned by the Democrats (Trump, 2020j). But in leaked videos of the February gatherings activists discussed how they were using the method to consolidate the Christian evangelical vote behind the Republicans. 'So our organization is going to be harvesting ballots in churches', said Ralph Reed, the chairman of the Faith and Freedom Coalition, to one meeting (in O'Harrow, 2020).

These assorted networks of religious conservative groups, who are closer to Vice-President Mike Pence than Trump himself, have a dominating position in the new, radical right

Republican Party. Trump is unlikely to have won the 2016 presidency without their energetic support. His commitment to place their supporters in the American judiciary was key to forging this alliance. Trump's team recognized in the summer of 2016 that without the support of the Christian right they could not sustain the core Republican vote. Pence, a Catholic-raised evangelical, known as one of the most religious members of Congress, suited this agenda. Crucially, they also publicized a list of potential Supreme Court nominations and an 'advisory board' on faith issues that were drawn directly from this milieu (Coppins, 2018). Pence's polite demeanour became a reassuring 'good cop'. But while these Christian activists may not have liked Trump's personal behaviour, or his occasionally leftist rhetoric, they were also firmly of the radical right. Indeed, the differences between Trumpism and this grouping can be overstated – and the danger that America faces in the future may well come from a polite, softly spoken authoritarianism and White supremacy, which calmly appeals to religious sanctity and morality.

Crucially, for this group Trump delivered on his side of the bargain. He made three Supreme Court appointments that replaced conservatives. The last was controversially pushed through on the eve of the presidential election with Amy Coney Barrett taking the seat of deceased liberal-feminist, Ruth Bader Ginsburg. Trump has also made nearly 200 further appointments to the federal judiciary, more than any previous president at the end of a first term. This means a quarter of sitting federal judges in the United States have been appointed by the Trump administration (Gramlich, 2020). The Council for National Policy provided the White House with information on the credentials of these appointees. They see this as a critical battle in the struggle to protect America's Christian values. Kelly Shackelford, who was name checked by Trump at the beginning of his keynote (Trump, 2020j), is the organization's vice president. He boasted of their successful lobbying and direct line to the president at the recorded events.

'Some of us literally opened a whole operation on judicial nominations and vetting ... We poured millions of dollars into this to make sure the president has good information ... picks the best judges', he said (in O'Harrow, 2020). These judges tend to be committed to a deeply conservative and religious jurisprudence. They are often attached to the legal doctrine known as 'originalism': the belief that the constitution's interpretation should not be updated but resemble as much as possible the arguments of the original 'Founding Fathers' in the 1780s – despite the huge social and cultural changes seen in the period since, not least the enfranchisement of women, the working classes and the end of slavery.

Barrett's selection has brought attention to bear on People of Praise, a tiny cross-denominational Christian organization with around 1,650 members who agree to live commune-like lives in the service of God. The organization has a strict view of heterosexual, traditional gender roles. Men are seen as the natural leaders of family life and it has an all-male leadership. The highest position a woman can hold is that of 'woman leader', which was previously referred to as a 'handmaid'. Barrett has not spoken publicly of her membership of People of Praise, but a list of members obtained by the *New York Times* describes her as one of 11 local 'leaders for women members' in South Bend (Dias et al, 2020). She is also on the board of a private school linked to the group that have a policy of not admitting children of unmarried parents and whose representatives have spoken out against gay marriage (Dias et al, 2020). These affiliations give a sense of the philosophy she will bring to the Court.

Predictably, Barrett aligns strongly with the anti-abortion rights sentiment of this milieu, which has long sought to overturn the 1973 *Roe* v *Wade* Supreme Court judgment. There are currently 15 bills at various stages of progression towards the Court. Some place such extreme restrictions on *Roe* v *Wade* rights that they come close to effectively overturning it – notably the so-called 'heartbeat bill' of the state of Georgia that would ban abortions beyond the stage of six weeks in all but exceptional circumstances. Similarly, the future of LGBT+ rights on the conservative court is uncertain. Some conservative judges have recently supported LGBT+ rights; notably, in the 2020 Supreme Court ruling that took the simple position that 'homosexuality or transgender status is not relevant to employment decisions'(Biskupic, 2020a), which was supported by Trump appointee, Neil Gorsuch, and Bush appointee, John Roberts. Barrett's views however are considered more hard-line than these judges (Moreau, 2018). Conservatives are also more united in opposing the landmark 2015 case on same-sex marriage rights with liberals now a bench minority (Resnick et al, 2015; Sherman and Gresko, 2020).

The Supreme Court is likely to now have a majority (possibly of 5 to 4 as Roberts is seen as more moderate and cautious) for a more politically interventionist, conservative court. Ideologically the justifications for this posture are drawn from the 'turn' in American conservatism we discussed in Chapter Two, which is perfectly encapsulated by the essay, *America Is a Republic, Not a Democracy* (Dobski, 2020). This uses the language of constitutionality to radically embrace minority rule. It occurs in the context where Republicans held a majority in the 2018–2020 Senate despite being elected by 15 million fewer Americans than their Democratic colleagues. It also builds upon a conservative grievance at what they allege has been decades of liberal activism on the Court, which has undermined the 'rights of states'. A testing ground for this 'interventionist' brand of judicial conservatism will be the Affordable Care Act (or 'Obamacare') that will shortly face its third Supreme Court challenge. In 2017, the Republicans failed to repeal the Bill in the Senate due to a rebellion on their own side. Polls show that a clear majority of Americans support the Bill and oppose a Supreme Court move against it. But ominously Barrett has a record of opposition to the ruling of the Court in relation to the Act (Biskupic, 2020b). Given that Trump failed in his bid to use democratic channels to overturn the legislation, despite the Senate's considerable bias towards the Republican Party, a judicial intervention would be hugely controversial – though early indications are that the Act will not be overturned completely.

Varieties of authoritarian protectionism

The Sino-America interrelationship adds further complexity to the ideological forms authoritarian protectionism assumes across different countries. In the US, it mobilizes the language of classical liberalism to oppose majoritarianism through an 'originalist' conception of the constitution. This appears, on the surface, quite different to the assertion of vulgar majoritarianism often found among the new right in Europe, notably in Hungary and Poland. But the distinction in language can be deceptive, as both these approaches see the legal system as a crucial means to entrench a politics of ultra-conservatism based on family, nation, tradition and Christian religiosity (Chapter Two). In each of these cases, politics is seen as a zero-sum game and battle of ideas based on highly partisan interests.

This views the political contest as civilizational and existential. Trump's brand of authoritarian protectionism contains this almost morbid sense of impending social collapse; a classic 'temporal emergency', a now or never contest to save the nation from a mortal danger. This is why it sits easily with the QAnon conspiracy theory that views Trump in millenarian terms, the last hope of America against a secret paedophile ring, which, it alleges, lies at the very heart of the country's establishment.

Trumpism is also highly de-institutional. He seeks to diminish public service bodies and has left hundreds of posts unfilled during his presidential tenure (Partnership for Public Service, nd). A report into Trump's management of the State Department described it as 'decimated' with a third of senior political appointments unappointed three and a half years into his presidency and a general chronic lack of staff and resources (Democratic Staff Report, 2020). He also pushed for huge cuts to the environmental agency – though these were partially obstructed by Congress (Scott, 2019). And has abolished 70 different environmental regulations (Popovich et al, 2020). So, Trump takes the ideology of low taxes, free markets and minimal government of Reaganite conservatism to a particularly dysfunctional extreme. These tax cuts have been financed by big increases in US federal debt. Even prior to the pandemic the US was heading to a normalized annual budget deficit of US$1 trillion (C. Jones, 2020).

So, this brand of authoritarianism pursues the de-institutionalization of the state, making it a site of rentier claims, not the delivery of public goods. This scaling back of state capacity renders populations more vulnerable, but goes alongside the aggressive language of national, partisan *protection*.

The Chinese variety under Xi Jinping adopts organizational assumptions that are very different to Trumpism. Its conception of the state is highly institutionalized, coordinated and asserts a dominating authority over the market. In the 'Chinese dream' the party represents the absolute interests of the nation in guiding the people towards their historical mission. The approach recalls the classical democratic deficiency of Leninism that was prophetically anticipated by the young Leon Trotsky in 1904, long before the brutalities of Stalin's dictatorship. 'In the internal politics of the Party these methods lead', he argued, 'to the Party organization "substituting" itself for the Party, the Central Committee substituting itself for the Party organization, and finally the dictator substituting himself for the Central Committee' (Trotsky, 1904). The secular religion of Xi Jinping Thought, which nominally acknowledges democracy as one among many 'core socialist values',[3] offers a similar series of displacements that result in a political system based on the absolute control of the leader over society.

The political insecurities of this increasingly totalitarian state is similar to that of all absolute monarchies. It requires equating the identity and interests of the leader with that of the nation; a move that is likely to be seen as implausible, ultimately illegitimate and based on weak moral foundations. In this context, authoritarian protectionism becomes particularly important due to this broader deficiency of legitimation that absolute imperial systems tend to have. It provides the homogenous identity and sense of partisan interests with which the leader claims to express the total will of the national people.

This cannot disguise however the very weak level of input legitimacy, even with innovations such as the social credit system that involve a quasi 'meritocratic' element. How long this system can be sustained on such a weak basis will therefore depend heavily on its ability to continue to offer output legitimacy: the extent to which the social contract based on rising living standards in China persists. This is one of the big open questions of the post-virus world – and early indications look very good for China's ruler. If China is able to continue to prosper, having successfully protected its citizens from COVID-19, while much of the rest of the world flounders with the disease and its fallout, then its star will further rise. The big danger for the regime in this scenario would be an excess of hubris; for example, overreaching in relation to its geopolitical goals in Taiwan following its successful repression in Hong Kong. After all, many imperial monarchies in history have misstepped badly when drunk on success.

SIX

Authoritarian Futures?

We should conceive of ourselves not as rulers of Earth, but
as highly powerful, conscious stewards. The Earth is given
to us in trust, and we can screw it up or make it work well
and sustainably.

Kim Stanley Robinson, speaking to
Wired *magazine, 2007*

The future of our democracy is at stake. The price of failure
is just too great to imagine.

Bernie Sanders, speech at the
2020 Democrat National Convention

Recall how, in Chapter Two, we observed that hegemony-
seeking actors have to engage in what Gramsci called 'mass
creation'. They have to resist merely declaring their own
'fanatical philosophical and religious convictions', and instead
formulate their ideas in a manner that suits their embedded-
ness in the broader body politic (Gramsci, 1971, p 341). The
'real critical test' (Gramsci, 1971, p 341) of any politics is the
extent to which they can build a genuine following for their
ideas among the public, in mass society. Gramsci distinguished
between 'arbitrary constructions', which do not find a foundation in real, living circumstances, and those 'which respond to
the demands of a complex organic period of history' (Gramsci,

1971, p 341). As this suggests, history is not a set of pure contingencies. It is not simply formed through the voluntaristic actions of individuals, either elites or insurgents, but is rather shaped by human social relations. This process includes the decisions and choices of individuals; the social structures like work, production and consumption that shape our material wellbeing; and the complex mix of social relations that form through the interactions of individual societies at the international level (on this see Lawson, 2006; Cooper, 2013). Historical change occurs through the combination of each of these elements. The changing social relations of capitalist economics are shaped by the uneven and combined interactions of societies and vice versa; while hegemony-seekers have to take stock of these conditions, make choices that reflect these circumstances and forces, but also seek to move beyond them. They ask how they can insert particular inputs that generate new outputs and change the overall trajectory of history.

Authoritarian protectionism offers a particularly regressive set of inputs that respond 'to the demands of a complex organic period of history' (Gramsci, 1971, p 341). To draw an analogy with the economic market, its success reflects a combination of supply and demand. In conditions of heightened crisis suppliers of 'blood and soil' narratives seeking political hegemony have found increased demand in the market for their ideas. Moreover, while the technological and social structures of work and production have changed enormously over the past 200 years, the primacy of nationality to political identity has not. It has been the unbroken thread across this long period. The enduring structure of nationality does not make the ethnonationalist politics of authoritarian protectionism inevitable. But it does provide a cultural environment, in which nationalism is always present as a latent possibility.

Authoritarian protectionists have already passed the test of 'organicity'. It has gone through the normalization Gramsci saw as the test of a hegemony-seeking political bloc. But drawing on the cases we have analysed, what can we conclude about its fundamental nature? In Chapter Two we also outlined the questions that Gramsci proposed scholars asked in order to develop a concrete analysis of the fascist movements of his own time. These sought to integrate the social, cultural and economic dimensions:

1. What is the social and class profile of those turning to the far right?
2. What impact has this new authoritarian bloc had on the rest of society as a whole? How has it changed the balance of forces?
3. What is the 'political and social significance' of the demands put forward by the movements' leaders which have found popular support? 'To what effective needs do they respond?'
4. How do the means the movement pursues relate to the supposed ends?
5. Is there a tension between the ends the followers expect and those that are likely? (Adapted from Gramsci, 1971, pp 166–167)

It is now possible to answers these questions more directly. Authoritarian protectionists respond to 'effective needs' (question five) at two levels. First, in domestic politics they offer the recognition of nativist grievances through the reassuring drumbeats of ethnonational identity. These 'needs' emerge on the demand side as rising inequality and a lack of economic insecurity connect to a politics of racial grievance, fear and a lost sense of entitlement. Authoritarian protectionists radically prioritize the recognition of nativist identity above all else. But they may also combine this with, at least, a rhetorical gesture towards some form of redistributional politics. With the transition from authoritarian individualism (with the stress on the importance of competition between individuals in the market) to authoritarian protectionism, the ideological narrative of the post-neoliberal right has moved towards a more collectivist discourse where membership of the in-group, the ethno-nation, confers distributional advantages *as a right*. While the extent to which this has occurred is uneven (the BJP in India may be distinctive for drawing on a more conditional, conventional Thatcherite discourse), the trend can be seen clearly in the cases of Orbán in Hungary, Kaczyński in Poland and Trump in the United States. Importantly, though they may deliver some limited redistributional outcomes, this is not decisive to the analysis. They simply need to gesture towards this ideologically. They assert the deep primacy of the collective as a guarantor of rights for the ethno-nation. But they do not seek to equalize the group. Their 'solidarity' has clear limits.

Second, in international politics, authoritarian protectionists respond highly effectively to the changing economic and political landscape of globalization. Since the 2008 global economic crisis the world system has experienced heightened competition between states. Conventional economic measures of globalization have contracted. In 2017, cross-border capital flows were 65 per cent below their 2008 level (Lund et al, 2017) and between 2014 and 2018 world trade grew at a lower level than economic growth – reversing decades of development in which the opposite had been the case (James, 2018, pp 221–222). Markets have also become more fragile and dependent on extensive state intervention. This was already the case after the 2008 financial crisis but has reached an unprecedented extent in the 2020 pandemic, which saw sweeping state intervention to underwrite the private sector. However, as we have noted, insofar as this serves to inflate asset prices it deepens inequality and does not deliver the structural reforms the economy needs. Perhaps more by accident than design, authoritarian protectionism emerges as a 'natural' governing logic in this context. It offers an identity politics of distraction in the face of rising economic inequalities – and while it may pursue non-neoliberal remedies to address these issues, it is too conservative to countenance any form of radical redistribution.

This makes them an attractive potential partner for the ultra-wealthy seeking to as far as possible to uphold the status quo order in monetary and economic policy.

The aggressive pursuit of ethnonational interests has negative implications for the multilateral system. In the context of falling trade and capital flows, conflict over the terms of trade has increased globally. Nonetheless, the stop–start trade war between China and the United States is an illustration of the limited character of these tensions to date. Even the most nationalistic president in modern American history prioritized certain areas of interest to his supporters, like pork tariffs to help farmers in the swing state of Iowa, over a full trade war (James, 2018, p 227). In Britain, Brexit brings a much greater breach in UK trade relations. But it has been incoherently pursued in the name of a supposedly 'free trade' agenda.

The political and social significance of authoritarian protectionism (also question five) is to put a roadblock in the way of the changes required to deal with the environmental and social challenges of the century. Indeed, authoritarian protectionism does not offer a degenerate utopia in the style of interwar fascism. It does not promise a 'new world', but instead represents a long-term corrosion of democratic practices and possibilities. The central position of national-ethnic identities in these worldviews, and the diminished status of other ideological beliefs, also allows for more heterodox alliances between states. As states are viewed as, above all, ethnic communities, their political complexion is often seen as irrelevant. In the Vietnamese context, for example, anti-Chinese sentiment defines the country's authoritarian protectionism. Many hold the short-lived Chinese incursion of 1979, and the decade of border clashes that followed, to have become a more significant event than the American war (Sullivan, 2015). Official and informal discourses situate China as 'the bad other' (Nguyen, 2017, p 34). The 2014 anti-Chinese riots fuelled by territorial disputes in the South China Sea are an example of this trend

(*BBC News*, 2014). Against this background a transactional international politics emerges, in which 'red' Vietnam actively sides with the United States against its communist neighbour, China. The almost entirely transactional conception of foreign policy used by the Trump administration, including his failed diplomatic initiative towards North Korea (Borger, 2019), can be viewed through the same lens. So, authoritarian protectionism as an external doctrine lacks any normative assessment of world politics. It gives first priority to bargains favourable to its own interests.

These means and ends (question four) point to the emergence of an unstable, fragile system of globalization with increased tensions over trade and economic governance. It sustains high levels of inequality by encouraging citizens to prioritize feelings of cultural, ethnic and national grievance. The search for hegemony in domestic politics seeks to build alliances through the use of 'shock and awe', 'spectacular' (Pulido et al, 2019) politics, cultivating an angry, sometimes street based fringe, and cohering a broader conservative alliance by stoking fear over their allegedly dangerous opponents. A cross–class alliance emerges under the banner of this agenda (question one). In some countries, even large parts of organized labour have responded positively. Trump, for example, won 40 per cent of the vote in labour union households at the 2020 election (*New York Times*, 2020b) – a slight fall on his 2016 performance (CNN, 2016). While generally this capacity to reach out across different classes has been a strength of the authoritarian protectionist appeal, when they fail to deliver for these voters it could become a weakness, undermining the credibility of their claim to take seriously these voters' demands (question five). And the likelihood of this occurring is also a warning. For the ethno-identity politics will only be pursued more trenchantly when they fail to materially protect the lives of 'their people'.

Authoritarian protectionists are, however, changing the balance of forces and trajectories of society in important ways (question two). Their desire to wield sovereignty autocratically makes them hostile to institutions and the rule of law. This opens up a breach with traditional neoliberalism. The British post-Thatcherites have not only largely abandoned the language of authoritarian individualism, they have also declared an offensive against the managerial bureaucracies they once backed to enforce their agenda. They railed against 'nightmarish procurement rules' (Cummings, 2016) imposed by the EU when outside of power. Once in government they took the opportunity to suspend these provisions. The result has been a series of 'cronyist' deals at great cost to the taxpayer. This is underpinned by a vision that treats the state as a platform-like organization distributing tenders to the private sector in a flexible way (Cummings, 2016). It allegedly creates responsive dynamism. But by removing regulatory checks from how power is wielded it encourages cronyism and corruption. At a time when markets are heavily state-reliant in order to function, this pushes authoritarian policy making in the direction of crony capitalism. A similar example lies in the British government's bid to extricate the UK from the EU state aid rules, which traditionally Thatcherites argued did not go far enough to protect 'free' competition. This agenda departs quite significantly from technocratic neoliberalism. They argue that freed from these rules the UK will be able to aggressively subsidize the tech sector in order to create Chinese and American style 'big data' multinationals. So, this assertion of sovereignty has led Brexiters to reject the neoliberal idea of a level playing field. They still believe in 'free trade' but have become pseudo-mercantilist in effect.

We can argue also that these trends are features of how authoritarian protectionism has re-politicized the use of power. Technocratic managerialism has been displaced by the hyper-ideological politics of 'them and us'. Once the partisan interests of supporters are given absolute importance it sits easily with an economics based on the distribution of rents. But American-style corporate capture – which is arguably what is unfolding in the British model, either by accident or design – is only one possible destination for this logic. In Hungary, Orbán's autocratic wielding of sovereignty has eroded the distinction between public and private. In this form, the state 'captures' business and society. Referred to as 'financial nationalism' (Johnson and Barnes, 2015) it sees the state strengthened in relation to the market, but in a highly clientelist form. Orbán has used EU-funded public procurement contracts without robust tendering processes to create a class of friendly oligarchs. They receive 90 per cent of their income from these contracts which are systematically over-priced (Corruption Research Centre Budapest, 2016, 2019; Magyar and Madlovics, 2019). Hungary's richest man today is Lőrinc Mészáros. A one-time gas fitter from Orbán's hometown, state contracts have turned him into a hugely wealthy individual. He is now number 2,057 on the Forbes Rich List (Forbes Rich List, 2020). Many Hungarian oppositionists believe he is merely the front-person for Orbán's personal fortune. Beyond the elite, Hungarian authoritarian protectionism has also been ideologically flexible. Orbán has been willing to mix austerity and patronage as required. He pushed through a windfall tax as part of the country's post-2008 crisis recovery, used government funding to create a slavishly pro-regime media landscape and pursued business-friendly policies, such as a flat rate tax (Bozóki, 2015, p 15). Breaking with neoliberal meritocracy, this sits easily with a claim to protect on the basis of ethnonational identity.

This shift towards crony capitalism under the auspices of a hyper-politicized, autocratic conception of sovereignty departs significantly from 'technocratic' neoliberal globalism. Trump wages war on institutions in the name of an autocratic sovereignty that prioritizes the distribution of rents to supporters. As we noted in Chapter Three, his one-time strategist, Steve Bannon, described this as a struggle to 'deconstruct … the administrative state' (cited in Michaels, 2017). China, by contrast, upholds a highly institutionalized autocracy. The country's approach to capital controls and state-run banking makes it distinctive as a great power that openly rejects many of the technocratic shibboleths of neoliberalism. In these different ways they illustrate a world in which autocratic politics is changing our economics. Despite their differences these forces are critical of the trade liberalization agenda. Instead, they seek out mercantilist advantages in a competitive world order.

If, however, we think of neoliberalism in broader terms, then we could see it as evolving, not dying. Accounts that draw on the work of Karl Polanyi (2001) show how it comprises 'a simultaneous roll-back *and roll-out* of state functions' (Peck, 2001, p 447, emphasis in original; see also Slobodian, 2018). Indeed, Polanyi argued that in principle an ultra 'free' market would require an authoritarian state to protect it. Hence the classical liberal belief in a 'pure' economic freedom was an illusion. In the real world, a politics that gave total priority to the freedoms of capital above all else would necessarily lead to dictatorial politics (Polanyi, 2001, pp 265–266). 'Liberal or neoliberal utopianism is [thus] doomed', writes David Harvey, 'to be frustrated by authoritarianism, or even outright fascism. The good freedoms are lost, the bad ones take over' (Harvey, 2007, p 37). First published during the Bush Jr administration, and prior to the financial crisis, Harvey's remarks today seem highly prescient. And if neoliberalism is viewed – as he argues – primarily as a process of restoring power to the financial class by opening up new areas for capitalist predation, then authoritarianism can clearly be its greatest ally.

A radical politics of survival towards a new democratic era

It has often been observed that Hollywood disaster movies in the 1990s predicted the crisis-wracked politics of the 21st century rather cogently. Uncontrollable pandemics, nationalism or religious extremism, and artificial intelligence (perhaps the crisis 'still to come') have been the subject of a number of apocalyptic movies. In this genre, the mid-1990s film, *12*

Monkeys, is notable for its catastrophic vision of a human species facing extinction after a pandemic. Despite the use of time travel the film's protagonist, James Cole, finds himself unable to save humanity from itself. No matter what course of action is taken, humanity is locked in a spiral to extinction. In this version of dystopia, there is no hope, only different vantage points in time to watch the end of the world. In a prescient commentary on the movie first published 18 months prior to the global pandemic, Abraham Riesman mused that 'it seems, these days, as though the human race has passed a Rubicon and is now on a straight path toward ... the end of the social order as we know it'. This has changed our sense of the past and future; 'our minds are situated in the years to come, as though we're already looking back on what's happening to us right now from the vantage point of the coming calamities' (Riesman, 2020).

Riesman captures how many of us feel about our apocalyptic era. Environmental calamities are a near-certainty in the future timeline of the 21st-century world. After all, even the most radical proposals for climate action are now mitigation efforts hoping to reduce, not negate, the crises ahead. 'The past' therefore has a tremendous determining role on the present and future. We cannot change it and have no choice but to deal with the inherited consequences of past human decisions. But this does not make the future timeline entirely determined. We can still make choices that can change our destiny. So, in this context, to refer to the rise of authoritarianism as contagion does not mean it is an unstoppable and overwhelming force in our politics. Rather, the metaphorical description has two implications. On the one hand, authoritarianism replicates in pathogen-like ways as it diffuses through the world system. Authoritarians become stronger when their co-thinkers in other states succeed. They can model their own efforts on these experiences, creating impetus and a sense of momentum. On the other hand, like pathogens the spread is not inevitable and can be stopped by effective political action. Studying and understanding the nature of the threat is an important part of democratic resistance.

The maxim, 'the world will end for others but not for us', expresses the crux of the opportunity for authoritarian protectionists in this century of unfolding crisis. Across 2020 the world's focus was naturally on the cataclysmic fallout from the global pandemic. But it was by no means the only sign of crisis in the human relation to nature evident across this difficult year. In California, there were a series of devastating wildfires, which followed an even more harrowing 'black summer' in Australia. Caused by drought and rising temperatures they were a grim indication of the scale of humanity's survival challenge. In the Californian case, the burnt area came to some 5,667 square miles – a territory so great it is equivalent in size to the 14 largest US cities combined (Peischel, 2020). These events also illustrated the ominous possibility of feedback loops that compound the basic problem of rising temperatures, catalysing further crises: 'California's wildfires release[ed] in six weeks what more than one million cars would release in a year, if each drove 11,500 miles in that period' (Peischel, 2020, np). As emissions and temperatures continue to rise the world has also grown used to 'first' occurrences. In one such sign of the future to come, the Laptev Sea in the Siberian Arctic had not begun freezing by the end of October 2020 – the first time this had happened since records began (Watts, 2020). Like other long crises in world history these ecological conditions shape the horizons of inter-human conflict. They raise the prospect of a series of catastrophic events, a major world city lost to fires or an entire country lost to flooding. The ecological crisis represents a moment of reckoning for the species. It posits the need for fundamental system change in how societies collect-ively organize their politics and economics.

Humanity's social structure seems particularly unprepared for the crises ahead. Unlike other ecologically derived long crises in human history, this one – as we have discussed – has been 'created' firmly in the structures of the social world: an economic system producing extremely high social inequality, unsustainable patterns of industrialization and consumption, and with geopolitical arrangements among states that are fracturing between big blocs with weak incentives for cooperation. As Polanyi warned, capital-centric systems – with very high amounts of economic 'freedom' for the holders of assets – create a trend line towards autocracy to protect the system from democratic demands. As all economies are now very dependent on the state, the question is not whether intervention should occur but what form it should take. The current model – ultra low interest rates, low levels of investment and declining productivity – has created a speculative 'rentier' economy that is highly dependent on state intervention. Indeed, during the 2020 crisis the small coterie of 2,189 dollar billionaires perversely saw their wealth increase by more than a quarter, reaching an all-time high of US$10.2 trillion (Neate, 2020). They already started the year with a wealth equivalent to the bottom 60 per cent of humanity (Oxfam International, 2020). As this state-supported, rentier system marches on it seems hardly surprising that a kleptocratic model of government with its politics of 'them and us' has proven to be highly attractive.

Facing these conditions authoritarian protectionism offers a message that combines exclusion with an ethnic 'solidarity'. Hope and salvation can be achieved for the community only if its foreign enemies – within and without – are vanquished and the alleged needs of the national people are given absolute priority. The core sociological condition for this political and ideological posture is the reality of a 'divided' humanity, separated out into a plethora of societies and identities, each interacting and conflicting. 'The world will end for others but not for us' feeds off the presence of the external 'other' against which the community's own identity and needs can be defined and 'upheld' against the rest.

Overcoming this is the central question facing a radical politics of survival: how can the scale of the system change needed be brought about in a world where universal, collective action is very difficult? Is the unevenness in the political development of states doomed to impair the universal, ecologically sustainable outcome needed? Unequal and ecologically damaging economic models have, after all, sat easily with the competitive logics of the nation-state system. Taken together they incentivize short-term, unjust outcomes over long-term, sustainable ones. So, what is a problem for a radical politics of survival is simultaneously the source of authoritarian protectionism's strength. It embraces and emphasizes a series of divisions that are already 'present' in the human sociology of planet Earth.

Yet, while these problems exist in international systems, we also have to find ways of working within this complex structure of the human world. Apart from their 'dark potentials' international systems also have positive qualities. From the diversity of human culture they contain, to the basis they provide for mutual learning through the diffusion of knowledge and replication of approaches pioneered elsewhere. One country's socioeconomic experiment can be another's inspiration or warning. So, while we can see the difficulties that international systems present for collective action on an issue like climate change, they also contain the basis to resolve it: pioneer states have to demonstrate what is possible and the positives change can bring to human wellbeing. While this dynamic of mutual learning and replication is currently benefiting the authoritarian right, an alternative strategy also needs to operate on this horizon. When ideas diffuse through international systems the models adjust to circumstance as societies modify, adapt and innovate. But perhaps the more challenging issue is how to address the real feelings of belonging and identity that are associated with the national community; a 'membership', as we saw Hobsbawm put it, that appears 'permanent, indestructible, and ... certain' (Hobsbawm, 1992, p 7). Although national identity is in part defined by who is 'not' included in the community, the non-national, this does not mean that a particular nation has to practice a policy of exclusion and aggression towards others. Nationality can often form unthreatening and benign registers of mutual attachment. Decades of multicultural evolution in many states have also demonstrated how nationality can be de-racialized. Meanwhile, even when nationality is politicized as nationalism it does not necessarily lead to exclusionary politics. In its civic forms it can be open to immigration and cosmopolitan in its ethos.

Authoritarian protectionists' first cry against their critics is the charge of treachery to the nation. The challenge for their opponents – which cannot be resolved in theory, but only practice – is how to disarm these attacks without endorsing, either explicitly or implicitly, their exclusionary agenda. Indeed, a simple way to think about a radical politics of survival is that it constitutes the opposite of authoritarian protectionism. Rather than homogenize the national community as the property of a single ethnic group, it promotes internationalism and solidarity among peoples and states. The politics of 'them and us' collapse, once we embrace this pluralistic solidarity. Partisan interests are, in turn, displaced by a universal interest that addresses the needs of the three dimensions: socioeconomic redistribution, ecologically sustainable transition and the need for a global order based on justice and cooperation. Yet, within this context, we still need to consider how to connect a sense of belonging – including national fidelity and solidarity – with pluralism and tolerance. This seems to be a key question for the left today.

While many have argued that a progressive politics of 'them and us' is possible – a 'left populism' (Mouffe, 2018) – this raises a problematic question regarding how we approach the role of democracy in a vision of transformative change. While the battle of ideas is a vital part of the democratic reflection, deliberation and argument, a politics of 'them and us' risks slipping easily into a 'battle of people'. For sure, there are interest groups that form abstract entities – for example, the fossil fuel industry or private equity sector – that a democratic process needs to reform out of existence. Divisions between classes also regularly spill over into struggle and resistance – strikes and protests of the exploited, using their collective power. But recognizing this does not further require the construction of counterposed, exclusive identities of 'them and us'. In Britain, the divide between 'Remainers' and 'Leavers' proved particularly damaging to the Remain side, for example. Once the question of whether or not to be a member of the EU ceased to be a normal policy issue, but instead became a matter of identity, it was very fertile ground for the cultivation of an authoritarian politics based on partisan interests ('the will of the people'). 'Them and us' notions do seem to posit this anti-democratic logic.

A progressive hegemonic approach therefore needs to construct alternative moral claims that combine a notion of belonging with an inclusive and pluralistic approach. This is a particular challenge when contesting authoritarian protectionism for the following reasons. Not all views *can* be considered morally legitimate and this places an inherent limit to pluralism. Contesting authoritarian protectionist claims also involves resisting the normalization of hardline ethnic nationalism, of insisting upon its illegitimacy. Moreover, in the current climate, it has become common to complain about 'polarization'. However, in a situation which sees authoritarianism on the march, then a divided country, with high levels of contestation of this offensive, is infinitely better than a populace that falls passively behind its agenda.

Groups that form around political ideologies always have to confront the task of building much broader coalitions. Trump would not have had the electoral success he did without building outwards. His hegemonic strategy combined a respectable posture with a hardline one tailored to different audiences. And it involved a series of easily understood arguments – however cynical, reactionary or hypocritical – about American society and how it needed to change.

The eclectic character of some of these gestures is a classic example of what Mouffe and Ernesto Laclau called 'a complementary and contingent operation' (Laclau and Mouffe,

2001), which knits together diverse elements into a common whole that still shares a sense of belonging and cohesion. As in other examples of authoritarian protectionism that have been electorally successful Trump's coalition efforts did not require compromising his politics. But, if anything, his language grew more radical over the lifetime of his presidency and especially during the summer of 2020. Johnson's 2019 general election campaign was similarly direct: there was little ambiguity over his agenda, the voter was able to connect values to policies, and he took a decisive position on an issue that divided the country. A strategy for a left counter-hegemony could do worse than use some of these methods: a clear argument, a very direct appeal, and a strong sense of purpose. This approach can be articulated entirely expunged of the divisive politics of 'them and us'.

The anti-democratic practices of authoritarian protectionism are derivative of their first principle and starting point: ethnic nationalism. This provides the basis on which partisan interests are constructed that justify 'lawless' attacks on the democratic process. So, the alternative has to make a case for global cooperation, recognizing that we can be both national and global citizens (Marsili and Milanese, 2018) – and, indeed, we must think of ourselves as the latter if we are to address the crises of our time. Democracy is key to this transformation. It requires linking the protection of formalized, institutionalized systems of representation and human rights with a substantive empowerment agenda that gives citizens more control over the forces shaping their lives. An ecological social contract will also need to be forged. This should start from the principle that the changes we are forced to make to our lives are compensated by a range of other improvements in our wellbeing. Radical economic redistribution is a vital part of a transition to a new human ecology, as we learn to live in different, more sustainable ways.

Recognizing that democracy has both formal (the rules and institutions governing democratic systems) and substantive (measures that allow citizens to have more control over their lives) elements is crucial to turning back the authoritarian tide. Ethnic nationalist arguments found a hearing in societies where racism is prevalent and racialized structures of power exist. Yet, we also need to reflect upon the conditions that allowed these racist and authoritarian values which were already latent within the population to become politically activated (on this in relation to Brexit see Shaw, 2020). In this sense, to break up the authoritarian electoral coalition in society requires recognizing that, while its leaders cast the group as ethnically homogenous with partisan interests, this is *factually* not the case. Like all forms of mass politics and sentiment the authoritarian base contains a broad range of people. Identifying and peeling away its 'softer' elements has a clear strategic importance for all efforts to defeat its march.

Ultimately, the main weapon we have at our disposal is democracy, especially in its substantive form: building a basis for empowerment, deliberation and participation in society. Output and input legitimacy are combined in this approach. It seeks to create institutions that deliver greater democratic control over the economic sphere, and not 'just' the redistribution of wealth. In other words, it points to recognizing that the scale of the crisis requires a profound shift in the social relations shaping the economic and ecological sphere and to build support for this change requires a new democratic era.

Notes

Chapter one

[1] In formal terms, this dates from the advent of women's suffrage with the 19th Amendment (1920). However, the Jim Crow Laws continued to disenfranchise the Black community in the South until the passage of the 1965 Voting Rights Act.

Chapter three

[1] It also has some parallels with the euphemism used by the mainland European far right, 'ethnopluralism' (see Chapter Two).

Chapter four

[1] Excluding Turkmenistan and North Korea, states that were both alleged to have 'secret' outbreaks, and including only full members of the United Nations.

Chapter five

[1] Among low-income White voters Clinton won 35.6 per cent and among White voters with high school qualifications or less she won 27 per cent (Stonecash, 2017, p 39).

[2] Not to be confused with the popular vote. This refers to the electoral college. For example, Trump won Pennsylvania narrowly but took all of the state's electoral college votes. Results like this in a handful of swing states meant that he was able to lose the national popular vote but still won the presidency.

[3] The list is: 'prosperity, democracy, civility, harmony, freedom, equality, justice, the rule of law, patriotism, dedication, integrity and friendship' (Xi, 2015, np).

References

Amadeo, K., 2020. The real reason American jobs are going to. *The Balance*. www.thebalance.com/u-s-china-trade-deficit-causes-effects-and-solutions-3306277 (accessed 21 October 2020).

Amos, O., 2020. Ten countries kept out Covid. But did they win? *BBC News*. www.bbc.co.uk/news/world-asia-53831063 (accessed 21 March 2021).

Anderson, B., 2006. *Imagined Communities: Reflections on the Origin and Spread of Nationalism*, 3rd edn. Verso, London.

Anievas, A., 2014. *Capital, the State, and War: Class Conflict and Geopolitics in the Thirty Years' Crisis, 1914–1945.* University of Michigan Press, Ann Arbor.

Antonucci, L., Horvath, L., Kutiyski, Y. and Krouwel, A., 2017. The malaise of the squeezed middle: Challenging the narrative of the 'left behind' Brexiter. *Competition and Change* 21, 211–229.

Appadurai, A., 2020. The nine lives of modernization theory. *Los Angeles Review of Books*. https://lareviewofbooks.org/article/the-nine-lives-of-modernization-theory/ (accessed 3 September 2020).

Arendt, H., 1973. *The Origins of Totalitarianism*. Houghton Mifflin Harcourt, Orlando.

Arendt, H., 2019. *The Human Condition*, 2nd edn. University of Chicago Press, Chicago and London.

Aristotle, 350 BC. *Politics*. Classics MIT.edu Archive. http://classics.mit.edu/Aristotle/politics.2.two.html (accessed 9 February 2021).

Associated Press, 2018. Treffen der Jungen Alternative: Gauland: NS-Zeit nur ein 'Vogelschiss in der Geschichte'. *Die Zeit*. www.zeit.de/news/2018-06/02/gauland-ns-zeit-nur-ein-vogelschiss-in-der-geschichte-180601-99-549766?utm_referrer=https%3A%2F%2Fwww.google.com%2F (accessed 21 March 2021).

Ayyub, R., 2020. The destruction of India's judicial independence is almost complete. *Washington Post*. www.washingtonpost.com/opinions/2020/03/24/destruction-indias-judicial-independence-is-almost-complete/ (accessed 21 March 2021).

Bangel, C., Blickle, P., Erdmann, E., Faigle, P., Loos, A., Stahnke, J., Tröger, J. and Venohr, S., 2019. Ost-West-Wanderung: Die Millionen, die gingen. *Die Zeit*. www.zeit.de/politik/deutschland/2019-05/ost-west-wanderung-abwanderung-ostdeutschland-umzug (accessed 21 March 2021).

Barnett, A., 2020. Out of the belly of hell: COVID-19 and the humanisation of globalisation. *openDemocracy*. www.opendemocracy.net/en/opendemocracyuk/out-belly-hell-shutdown-and-humanisation-globalisation/ (accessed 8 July 2020).

BBC News, 2014. Factories burnt in Vietnam-China row. www.bbc.co.uk/news/world-asia-27403851 (accessed 21 March 2021).

BBC News, 2019. Hong Kong protests: President Xi warns of 'bodies smashed'. www.bbc.co.uk/news/world-asia-china-50035229 (accessed 21 March 2021)

BBC News, 2020a. Polish election: Andrzej Duda says LGBT 'ideology' worse than communism. www.bbc.co.uk/news/world-europe-53039864 (accessed 21 March 2021).

BBC News, 2020b. Hungary 'broke EU law with foreign funding rules'. www.bbc.co.uk/news/world-europe-53093117 (accessed 21 March 2021).

BBC News, 2020c. 'We live in a land of liberty' [Tweet]. Twitter. https://twitter.com/BBCNews/status/1240336719100227584 (accessed 21 August 2020).

BBC News, 2020d. Coronavirus: Brazil's Bolsonaro joins anti-lockdown protests. www.bbc.co.uk/news/world-latin-america-52351636 (accessed 21 March 2021)

Belich, J., 2016. The Black Death and the spread of Europe, in Belich, J., Darwin, J., Frenz, M., and Wickham, C. (eds), *The Prospect of Global History*. Oxford University Press, Oxford, pp 93–107.

Bender, J. 2017. AfD teilt aus: Gauland: Özoguz in Anatolien entsorgen. FAZ.NET. faz.net/aktuell/politik/bundestagswahl/afd-alexander-gauland-traeumt-von-entsorgung-aydan-oezoguz-15171141.html (accessed 21 March 2021).

Bender, J., 2018. AfD-Chef im Interview: Gauland für 'friedliche Revolution' gegen das 'politische System'. Faz.net. www.faz.net/aktuell/politik/inland/afd-chef-gauland-friedliche-revolution-gegen-das-politische-system-15771150.html (accessed 21 March 2021).

Bennett, J.T., 2020. Trump says Easter with 'packed churches' would be 'beautiful time' to reopen US. www.independent.co.uk/news/world/americas/us-politics/trump-coronavirus-news-reopen-us-borders-easter-holiday-a9423041.html (accessed 9 September 2020).

Berhe, M.G., 2020. *Laying the Past to Rest: The EPRDF and the Challenges of Ethiopian State-Building*. C. Hurst & Co., London.

Bermeo, N., 2016. On democratic backsliding. *Journal of Democracy* 27, 5–19.

Bethea, C., 2021. The Georgia dad who said that he wanted to kill Nancy Pelosi. *The New Yorker*. www.newyorker.com/news/us-journal/the-georgia-dad-who-said-that-he-wanted-to-kill-nancy-pelosi (accessed 2 February 2021).

Bieber, F., 2020. Global nationalism in times of the COVID-19 pandemic. *Nationalities Papers*, 1–13.

Biskupic, J., 2020a. Two conservative justices joined decision expanding LGBTQ rights. *CNN*. www.cnn.com/2020/06/15/politics/supreme-court-expanding-gay-rights/index.html (accessed 27 October 2020).

Biskupic, J., 2020b. What Amy Coney Barrett could mean for Obamacare. *CNN*. www.cnn.com/2020/10/10/politics/affordable-care-act-amy-coney-barrett-obamacare/index.html (accessed 27 October 2020).

Bloomenthal, A., 2020. World's top 10 internet companies. *Investopedia*. www.investopedia.com/articles/personal-finance/030415/worlds-top-10-internet-companies.asp (accessed 23 October 2020).

Boadle, A., 2020. Brazil's Bolsonaro militarizes his inner Cabinet. *Reuters*. www.reuters.com/article/us-brazil-politics-idUSKBN2072S5 (accessed 21 March 2021).

Borger, J., 2019. Donald Trump hails 'great leader' Kim Jong-un at Hanoi summit. *The Guardian*. www.theguardian.com/us-news/2019/feb/27/donald-trump-hails-great-leader-kim-jong-un-at-hanoi-summit (accessed 21 March 2021).

Bozóki, A., 2011. Occupy the state: The Orbán regime in Hungary. *Debatte: Journal of Contemporary Central and Eastern Europe* 19, 649–663.

Bozóki, A., 2015. Broken democracy, predatory state, and nationalist populism, in P. Krasztev and J.V. Til (eds), *The Hungarian Patient: Social Opposition to an Illiberal Democracy*. Central European University Press, Budapest, pp 3–36.

Bryant, M., 2020. Republican senator says 'democracy isn't the objective' of US system. *The Guardian*. www.theguardian.com/us-news/2020/oct/08/republican-us-senator-mike-lee-democracy (accessed 21 March 2021).

Bullough, O., 2018. *Moneyland: Why Thieves and Crooks Now Rule the World and How to Take it Back*. Profile Books, London.

Buras, P., 2019. The EU must defend its rule-of-law revolution. *Balkan Insight*. https://balkaninsight.com/2019/07/11/the-eu-must-defend-its-rule-of-law-revolution/ (accessed 15 October 2020).

Buras, P. and Knaus, G., 2018. Where the law ends: The collapse of the rule of law in Poland – and what to do. European Stability Initiative, Stefan Batori Foundation, Berlin and Warsaw.

Butcher, J., 2019. Brexit: Working class revolt or middle class outlook? *Discover Society*. https://discoversociety.org/2019/07/03/brexit-working-class-revolt-or-middle-class-outlook/ (accessed 15 October 2020).

Buzan, B. and Lawson, G., 2015. *The Global Transformation: History, Modernity and the Making of International Relations*. Cambridge University Press, Cambridge and New York.

Chacko, P., 2018. The right turn in India: Authoritarianism, populism and neoliberalisation. *Journal of Contemporary Asia* 48, 541–565.

Chacko, P., 2020. Gender and authoritarian populism: Empowerment, protection, and the politics of resentful aspiration in India. *Critical Asian Studies* 52, 204–225.

Chatterji, A.P., Hansen, T.B. and Jaffrelot, C., 2019. *Majoritarian State: How Hindu Nationalism is Changing India*. Oxford University Press, Oxford.

Chatterjee, P., 1991. Whose imagined community? *Millennium – Journal of International Studies* 20, 521–525.

Cheng, K., 2018. Interview: Labelled a 'threat to China', Hong Kong law scholar Benny Tai says Beijing is trying to brainwash Hongkongers. *Hong Kong Free Press*. https://hongkongfp.com/2018/04/12/interview-labelled-threat-china-hong-kong-law-scholar-benny-tai-says-beijing-trying-brainwash-hongkongers/ (accessed 22 October 2020).

Christopherson, S., Garretsen, H. and Martin, R., 2008. The world is not flat: Putting globalization in its place. *Cambridge Journal of Regions, Economy and Society* 1, 343–349.

ClimateTracker.org, 2020. Temperatures. *Climate Action Tracker*. https://climateactiontracker.org/global/temperatures/ (accessed 7 October 2020).

Cline, E.H., 2015. *1177 B.C.: The Year Civilization Collapsed*. Princeton University Press, Princeton.

CNN, 2016. 2016 election results: Exit polls. *CNN.com*. http://2016.elections.cnn.com/election/2016/results/exit-polls (accessed 6 November 2020).

Cohen, J., 2020. The coronavirus seems unstoppable. What should the world do now? *Science*. www.sciencemag.org/news/2020/02/coronavirus-seems-unstoppable-what-should-world-do-now (accessed 19 August 2020).

Colantone, I. and Stanig, P., 2018. Global competition and Brexit. *American Political Science Review* 112, 201–218.

Committee of Five, 1776. *Declaration of Independence: A Transcription*. National Archives. www.archives.gov/founding-docs/declaration-transcript (accessed 2 February 2021).

Cooper, L., 2013. Can contingency be 'internalised' into the bounds of theory? Critical realism, the philosophy of internal relations, and the solution of 'uneven and combined development'. *Cambridge Review of International Affairs* 26, 573–597.

Cooper, L. and Cooper, C., 2020. 'Get Brexit done': The new political divides of England and Wales at the 2019 election. *The Political Quarterly* 91:4. 751–761.

Cooper, L. and Molkenbur, T., 2019. *We the People? Dangers and Lessons for Europe on the Rise of the AfD in Germany*. LSE CCS, London.

Coppins, M., 2018. God's plan for Mike Pence. *The Atlantic*. www.theatlantic.com/magazine/archive/2018/01/gods-plan-for-mike-pence/546569/ (accessed 21 March 2021).

Corruption Research Centre Budapest, 2016. The detection of overpricing at EU funded public procurement in Hungary. www.crcb.eu/?p=1076 (accessed 13 January 2020).

Corruption Research Centre Budapest, 2019. The EU funds, Viktor Orbán, and Lőrinc Mészáros, the Hungarian gas fitter. www.crcb.eu/?p=1791 (accessed 13 January 2020).

Cragg, G., 2019. Poland woos voters with controversial child benefit scheme. *France 24*. www.france24.com/en/20190507-poland-woos-voters-controversial-child-benefits-scheme-european-union (accessed 14 October 2020).

Crouch, C., 2004. *Post-democracy*, 1st edn. Polity Press, Malden.

C-Span, 2020. President Trump walks across Lafayette Park to St. John's Church. www.youtube.com/watch?v=5ShnqmiKLE8 (accessed 21 March 2021).

Cummings, D., 2016. Dominic Cummings – Brexit Hearing 2016 – Part 01. www.youtube.com/watch?v=O50yPxXKTek (accessed 21 March 2021).

Davies, C., 2018. *Hostile Takeover: How Law and Justice Captured Poland's Courts*. Freedom House, Warsaw.

Davies, W., 2020. *This is Not Normal: The Collapse of Liberal Britain*. Verso, London and New York.

Davis, M., 2020. *The Monster Enters: COVID-19 and the Plagues of Capitalism*. OR Books, New York and London.

de Waal, A., 2015. *The Real Politics of the Horn of Africa: Money, War and the Business of Power*. Polity Press, Cambridge, UK and Malden, MA.

Decker, F., 2018. Wahlergebnisse und Wählerschaft der AfD | Parteien in Deutschland. bpb.de. www.bpb.de/politik/grundfragen/parteien-in-deutschland/afd/273131/wahlergebnisse-und-waehlerschaft (accessed 12 February 2021).

Democratic Staff Report, 2020. *Diplomacy in Crisis: The Trump Administration's Decimation of the State Department*. Prepared for the use of the Committee on Foreign Relations United States Senate.

Derrida, J., 2005. *Rogues: Two Essays on Reason*. Stanford University Press, Stanford.

Dias, E., Ruiz, R.R. and LaFraniere, S., 2020. Court nominee is conservative rooted in faith. *New York Times*, 11 October.

Die Welt, 2018. Für Höcke für Islam am Bosporus Schluss sein. www.welt.de/regionales/thueringen/article172946155/Fuer-Hoecke-fuer-Islam-am-Bosporus-Schluss-sein.html (accessed 21 March 2021).

Dijkstra, L., Poelman, H. and Rodríguez-Pose, A., 2020. The geography of EU discontent. *Regional Studies* 54:6, 737–753.

Dobski, B., 2020. *America Is a Republic, Not a Democracy*. The Heritage Foundation, Washington.

Drake, B.L., 2012. The influence of climatic change on the Late Bronze Age Collapse and the Greek Dark Ages. *Journal of Archaeological Science* 39, 1862–1870.

Drucker, J. and Lipton, E., 2019. How a Trump tax break to help poor communities became a windfall for the rich *New York Times*. www.nytimes.com/2019/08/31/business/tax-opportunity-zones.html (accessed 21 March 2021).

Economy, E.C., 2018. *The Third Revolution: Xi Jinping and the New Chinese State*. Oxford University Press, Oxford.

Fagan, B., 2001. *The Little Ice Age: How Climate Made History 1300–1850*. Basic Books, New York.

Farage, N., 2020. Coronavirus has shown we are all nationalists now. Does Boris Johnson realise that? *The Telegraph*. www.telegraph. co.uk/politics/2020/03/12/coronavirus-has-shown-nationalists-now-does-boris-johnson-realise/ (accessed 21 March 2021).

Farm Animal Investment Risk and Return, 2017. Factory farming in Asia: Assessing investment risks. *FAIRR*. www.fairr.org/article/ factory-farming-in-asia-assessing-investment-risks/ (accessed 1 September 2020).

Federici, S., 2004. *Caliban and the Witch: Women, the Body and Primitive Accumulation*, revised edn. Autonomedia, New York.

Finnigan, C., 2019. BJP's 2019 victory: How caste-based politics has been redefined and reinvented. *South Asia@LSE*. https://blogs. lse.ac.uk/southasia/2019/06/26/bjps-2019-victory-how-caste-based-politics-has-been-redefined-and-reinvented/ (accessed 5 February 2021).

Fischer, K., 2009. The influence of neoliberals before, during and after Pinochet, in P. Mirowski and D. Plehwe (eds), *The Road from Mont Pèlerin*. Harvard University Press, Cambridge, MA, pp 305–346.

Forbes Rich List, 2020. Lorinc Meszaros. *Forbes*. www.forbes.com/ profile/lorinc-meszaros/ (accessed 13 January 2020).

Fraser, N., 1995. From redistribution to recognition? Dilemmas of justice in a 'Post-Socialist' age. *New Left Review*, 1/212, 68–93.

Fraser, N., 2019. *The Old is Dying and the New Cannot be Born: From Progressive Neoliberalism to Trump and Beyond*. Verso Books, London and New York.

Freedom House, 2019. *Freedom in the World 2019: Democracy in Retreat*. Freedom House, Washington DC.

Friedman, T.L., 2007. *The World is Flat: The Globalized World in the Twenty-first Century*, 2nd revised edition. Picador, New York.

Gilbert, L. and Mohseni, P., 2011. Beyond authoritarianism: The conceptualization of hybrid regimes. *Studies in Comparative International Development* 46, 270.

Glenny, M., 2017. *McMafia: Seriously Organised Crime*, ebook edn. Vintage, London.

Goldstone, J.A., 1988. East and west in the seventeenth century: Political crises in Stuart England, Ottoman Turkey, and Ming China. *Comparative Studies in Society and History* 30, 103–142.

Goldstone, J.A., 1998. Initial conditions, general laws, path dependence, and explanation in historical sociology. *American Journal of Sociology* 104, 829–845.

Gopal, P., 2020. Coronavirus lockdown: Is Modi's India lurching towards fascism? *Another Europe* [podcast], EP55.

Gowan, P., 1999. *The Global Gamble: Washington's Faustian Bid for World Dominance*, 1st edn. Verso Books, London and New York.

Gramlich, J., 2020. How Trump compares with other recent presidents in appointing federal judges. *Pew Research Center*. www.pewresearch.org/fact-tank/2020/07/15/how-trump-compares-with-other-recent-presidents-in-appointing-federal-judges/ (accessed 6 November 2020).

Gramsci, A., 1971. *Selections from the Prison Notebooks*. International Publishers, New York.

Gross, S., 2020. What is the Trump administration's track record on the environment? Brookings. www.brookings.edu/policy2020/votervital/what-is-the-trump-administrations-track-record-on-the-environment/ (accessed 28 August 2020).

Grzebalska, W. and Pető, A., 2018. The gendered modus operandi of the illiberal transformation in Hungary and Poland. *Women's Studies International Forum* 68, 164–172.

Habermas, J., 1991. *The Structural Transformation of the Public Sphere: Inquiry into a Category of Bourgeois Society*, paperback edn. MIT Press, Cambridge, MA.

Hall, S., 1988. *The Hard Road to Renewal: Thatcherism and the Crisis of the Left*. Verso Books, London and New York.

Hall, S., 1998. The great moving nowhere show. *Marxism Today* special edition, 9–14.

Happy Planet Index, 2016. Vietnam country data. http://happyplanetindex.org/countries/vietnam (accessed 24 August 2020).

Harsin, J., 2020. Toxic white masculinity, post-truth politics and the COVID-19 infodemic. *European Journal of Cultural Studies*, 23:6, 1060-1068.

Harvey, D., 2007. *A Brief History of Neoliberalism*, new edn. Oxford University Press, Oxford.

Highmore, C.J., Warner, J.C., Rothwell, S.D., Wilks, S.A. and Keevil, C.W., 2018. Viable but nonculturable *Listeria monocytogenes* and *Salmonella enterica* serovar Thompson induced by chlorine stress remain infectious. *mBio* 9, 1–12.

Hinde, W., 1987. *Richard Cobden: A Victorian Outsider*, 1st edn. Yale University Press, New Haven.

Hobsbawm, E.J., 1992. Ethnicity and nationalism in Europe today. *Anthropology Today* 8, 3–8.

Hobsbawm, E.J., 1995. *Age of Extremes: The Short Twentieth Century, 1914–1991*. Abacus Books, London.

Hopkin, J., 2020. *Anti-System Politics: The Crisis of Market Liberalism in Rich Democracies*. Oxford University Press, Oxford and New York.

Hoyle, B. and Spencer, R., 2020. Coronavirus: Trump rejects idea of a nationwide lockdown. www.thetimes.co.uk/article/coronavirus-trump-rejects-idea-of-a-nationwide-lockdown-plw8cdhvz (accessed 21 March 2021).

Human Rights Watch, 2020. Vietnam: Crackdown on peaceful dissent intensifies. *Human Rights Watch*. www.hrw.org/news/2020/06/19/vietnam-crackdown-peaceful-dissent-intensifies (accessed 24 August 2020).

Hunt, J., 1990. Swift action call on 'greenhouse' gases; US doubt over evidence on global warming may leave it isolated at conference on climate change. *Financial Times*, 5 November 1990.

Hunter, W. and Power, T.J., 2019. Bolsonaro and Brazil's illiberal backlash. *Journal of Democracy* 30, 68–82.

IPCC, 2020. Statement on the 30th anniversary of the IPCC First Assessment Report – IPCC. Intergovernmental Panel on Climate Change. www.ipcc.ch/2020/08/31/st-30th-anniversary-far/ (accessed 7 October 2020).

James, H., 2018. Deglobalization: The rise of disembedded unilateralism. *Annual Review of Financial Economics* 10, 219–237.

Jennings, W. and Stoker, G., 2019. The divergent dynamics of cities and towns: Geographical polarisation and Brexit. *The Political Quarterly* 90, 155–166.

Johns Hopkins University Coronavirus Resource Centre, 2020. Johns Hopkins University COVID-19 Map and Resource Centre. JHU.Edu. https://coronavirus.jhu.edu/map.html (accessed 1 September 2020).

Johnson, B., 2020. Watch again: Boris Johnson tells pubs, bars, clubs and restaurants to close from Friday evening. Telegraph YouTube Channel. www.youtube.com/watch?v=oNkCuotL2TM (accessed 21 March 2021).

Johnson, J. and Barnes, A., 2015. Financial nationalism and its international enablers: The Hungarian experience. *Review of International Political Economy* 22, 535–569.

Jones, A., 2020. How 'overreaction' made Vietnam a virus success. *BBC News*. www.bbc.co.uk/news/world-asia-52628283 (accessed 21 March 2021).

Jones, C., 2020. Trump's deficits are racing past Obama's. *Forbes*. www.forbes.com/sites/chuckjones/2020/02/01/trumps-deficits-are-racing-past-obamas/ (accessed 28 October 2020).

Jones, D.S., 2014. *Masters of the Universe: Hayek, Friedman, and the Birth of Neoliberal Politics: Hayek, Friedman, and the Birth of Neoliberal*, updated edn. Princeton University Press, Princeton and Oxford.

Kaldor, M. and Vejvoda, I., 2002. *Democratization in Central and Eastern Europe*. Bloomsbury Publishing, London.

Kamann, M., 2017. AfD: Was Björn Höcke mit 'Denkmal der Schande'-Rede bezweckt. *Die Welt*. www.welt.de/politik/deutschland/article161286915/Was-Hoecke-mit-der-Denkmal-der-Schande-Rede-bezweckt.html (accessed 21 March 2021).

Kaniewski, D., Paulissen, E., Van Campo, E., Weiss, H., Otto, T., Bretschneider, J. and Van Lerberghe, K., 2010. Late second–early first millennium BC abrupt climate changes in coastal Syria and their possible significance for the history of the Eastern Mediterranean. *Quaternary Research* 74, 207–215.

Keane, J., 2020. *The New Despotism.* Harvard University Press, Cambridge, MA.

Kennedy, P., 1989. *The Rise and Fall of the Great Powers: Economic Change and Military Conflict from 1500–2000.* Fontana Press, London.

Khokhar, T., 2017. Chart: Global CO2 emissions rose 60% between 1990 and 2013. https://blogs.worldbank.org/opendata/chart-global-co2-emissions-rose-60-between-1990-and-2013 (accessed 7 October 2020).

Kimmel, M., 2013. *Angry White Men: American Masculinity at the End of an Era.* Nation Books, New York.

Kimmel, M. and Wade, L., 2018. Ask a feminist: Michael Kimmel and Lisa Wade discuss toxic masculinity. *Signs: Journal of Women in Culture and Society* 44, 233–254.

Knapp, A.B. and Manning, S.W., 2016. Crisis in context: The end of the Late Bronze Age in the Eastern Mediterranean. *American Journal of Archaeology* 120, 99–149.

Kornhauser, W., 2013. *Politics of Mass Society.* Routledge, Abingdon and New York.

Kostka, G., 2019. China's social credit systems and public opinion: Explaining high levels of approval. *New Media and Society* 21, 1565–1593.

Krastev, I., 2018. Eastern Europe's illiberal revolution: The long road to democratic decline. *Foreign Affairs* 97, 49–59.

Kurki, M. and Rosenberg, J., 2020. Multiplicity: A new common ground for international theory? *Globalizations* 17, 397–403.

Laclau, E. and Mouffe, C., 2001. *Hegemony and Socialist Strategy: Towards a Radical Democratic Politics,* 2nd revised edn. Verso Books, London and New York.

Lam, W. and Cooper, L. (eds), 2017. *Citizenship, Identity and Social Movements in the New Hong Kong: Localism after the Umbrella Movement.* Routledge, London and New York.

Lawson, G., 2006. The promise of historical sociology in international relations. *International Studies Review* 8, 397–423.

Layser, M.D., 2019. The pro-gentrification origins of place-based investment tax incentives and a path toward community oriented reform. *Wisconsin Law Review*, 745–818.

Leamer, E.E., 2007. A flat world, a level playing field, a small world after all, or none of the above? A review of Thomas L Friedman's *The World is Flat. Journal of Economic Literature* 45, 83–126.

Lindaman, D. and Viala-Gaudefroy, J., 2020. Donald Trump's 'Chinese virus': The politics of naming. *The Conversation.* http://theconversation.com/donald-trumps-chinese-virus-the-politics-of-naming-136796 (accessed 9 September 2020).

Lopez, G., 2016. Donald Trump's long history of racism, from the 1970s to 2019. *Vox.* www.vox.com/2016/7/25/12270880/donald-trump-racist-racism-history (accessed 28 February 2020).

Lopez, L., 2017. The White House is only telling you half of the sad story of what happened to American jobs. *Business Insider.* www.businessinsider.com/what-happened-to-american-jobs-in-the-80s-2017-7 (accessed 23 October 2020).

Luce, E., 2020. Will America tear itself apart? The Supreme Court, 2020 elections and a looming constitutional crisis. *Financial Times.* www.ft.com/content/b159bce5-83e7-4f8e-ab0d-4123660ab539 (accessed 16 October 2020).

Lund, S., Windhagen, E., Manyika, J., Härle, P., Woetzel, J. and Goldshtein, D., 2017. The new dynamics of financial globalization. McKinsey and Company. https://view.ceros.com/mckinsey/financial-globalization-v1 (accessed 2 November 2020).

Magyar, B. and Madlovics, B., 2019. Hungary's mafia state fights for impunity. *Balkan Insight.* https://balkaninsight.com/2019/06/21/hungarys-mafia-state-fights-for-impunity/ (accessed 10 January 2020).

Mahers, M., 2020. 'Standing by, sir': Proud Boys respond to Trump presidential debate mention. *The Independent.* www.independent.co.uk/news/world/americas/trump-presidential-debate-proud-boys-us-election-hate-group-b716510.html (accessed 9 February 2021).

Mahler, J., 2018. How one conservative think tank is stocking Trump's government. *New York Times*. www.nytimes.com/2018/06/20/magazine/trump-government-heritage-foundation-think-tank.html (accessed 21 March 2021).

Mahoney, J., 2000. Path dependence in historical sociology. *Theory and Society* 29, 507–548.

Mair, P., 2013. *Ruling the Void: The Hollowing of Western Democracy*. Verso, London and New York.

Marsili, L. and Milanese, N., 2018. *Citizens of Nowhere: How Europe Can Be Saved from Itself.* Zed Books, London.

Mason, P., 2019. *Clear Bright Future: A Radical Defence of the Human Being*. Allen Lane, London.

Mayer, M., 2018. China's historical statecraft and the return of history. *International Affairs* 94, 1217–1235.

McArthur, N., 2007. *David Hume's Political Theory: Law, Commerce, and the Constitution of Government*. University of Toronto Press, Toronto and Buffalo.

McFarlane, L., 2020. A spectre is haunting the West – the spectre of authoritarian capitalism. *openDemocracy*. www.opendemocracy.net/en/oureconomy/a-spectre-is-haunting-the-west-the-spectre-of-authoritarian-capitalism/ (accessed 29 April 2020).

Mechkova, V., Lührmann, A. and Lindberg, S.I., 2017. How much democratic backsliding? *Journal of Democracy* 28, 162–169.

Michaels, J., 2017. How Trump is dismantling a pillar of the American state. *The Guardian*. www.theguardian.com/commentisfree/2017/nov/07/donald-trump-dismantling-american-administrative-state (accessed 21 March 2021).

Mill, J.S., 1977. De Tocqueville on democracy in America, in *The Collected Works of John Stuart Mill, Volume XVIII – Essays on Politics and Society Part I (On Liberty)*. Liberty Fund Online Library of Liberty. https://oll.libertyfund.org/titles/mill-the-collected-works-of-john-stuart-mill-volume-xviii-essays-on-politics-and-society-part-i#lf0223-18_head_045 (accessed 21 March 2021).

Mill, J.S., 1989. *J.S. Mill: 'On Liberty' and Other Writings*. Cambridge University Press, Cambridge.

Mill, J.S., 2019. *Considerations on Representative Government*. Anodos Books, Dumfries and Galloway.

Mishra, P., 2020. Flailing states. *London Review of Books* 42:14. www.lrb.co.uk/the-paper/v42/n14/pankaj-mishra/flailing-states (accessed 21 March 2021).

Mondon, A. and Winter, A., 2020. *Reactionary Democracy: How Racism and the Populist Far Right Became Mainstream*. Verso Books, Brooklyn.

Moreau, J., 2018. Trump's Supreme Court shortlist alarms LGBTQ advocates. *NBC News*. www.nbcnews.com/feature/nbc-out/trump-s-extreme-supreme-court-shortlist-alarms-lgbtq-advocates-n889731 (accessed 26 October 2020).

Morse, Y.L., 2012. The era of electoral authoritarianism. *World Politics* 64, 161–198.

Mouffe, C., 2005. *On the Political*, 1st edn. Routledge, London and New York.

Mouffe, C., 2009. *The Democratic Paradox*. Verso, London.

Mouffe, C., 2018. *For a Left Populism*. Verso, London.

Mudde, C., 2019. *The Far Right Today*, iBook edn. Polity, Cambridge.

Mudde, C. and Kaltwasser, C.R., 2017. *Populism: A Very Short Introduction*. Oxford University Press, Oxford.

Muis, J. and Immerzeel, T., 2017. Causes and consequences of the rise of populist radical right parties and movements in Europe. *Current Sociology* 65, 909–930.

Muro, M. and Liu, S., 2016. Another Clinton-Trump divide: High-output America vs low-output America. Brookings Institute. www.brookings.edu/blog/the-avenue/2016/11/29/another-clinton-trump-divide-high-output-america-vs-low-output-america/ (accessed 28 August 2020).

Mustian, J., Flaccus, G., Kunzelman, M. and Biesecker, M., 2021. Who were they? Records reveal Trump fans who stormed Capitol. *AP News*. https://apnews.com/article/us-capitol-siege-trump-supporters-8edfd3bb994568b7cdcd2243ad769101 (accessed 2 February 2021).

Neate, R., 2020. Billionaires' wealth rises to $10.2 trillion amid Covid crisis. *The Guardian*. www.theguardian.com/business/2020/oct/ 07/covid-19-crisis-boosts-the-fortunes-of-worlds-billionaires (accessed 2 November 2020).

Never Again, 2020. The virus of hate: A selection of xenophobic incidents documented by the 'NEVER AGAIN' Association in the context of the coronavirus epidemic in 2020. Warsaw. www. nigdywiecej.org/en/ (accessed 22 April 2021).

New York Times, 2020a. 158 million Americans told to stay home, but Trump pledges to keep it short. www.nytimes.com/2020/ 03/23/world/coronavirus-updates-usa-world.html (accessed 21 March 2021).

New York Times, 2020b. National exit polls: How different groups voted. www.nytimes.com/interactive/2020/11/03/us/elections/ exit-polls-president.html (21 March 2021).

Newsweek Poland, 2017. 'Nie złamią nas' mówi Szydło w wywiadzie i każdą krytykę rządu uznaje za 'atak'. Newsweek.pl. www. newsweek.pl/polska/polityka/beata-szydlo-o-uchodzcach-wywiad-dla-tygodnika-sieci-prawdy/8km8ex6 (accessed 6 August 2020).

Nguyen, N.H.T., 2017. Anti-Chinese sentiment in contemporary Vietnam: Constructing nationalism, new democracy, and the use of 'the other'. Trinity University Digital Commons – Undergraduate Student Research Awards.

Nicolaidis, K., Gartzou-Katsouyanni, K. and Sternberg, C., 2018. *The Greco-German Affair in the Euro Crisis: Mutual Recognition Lost?* Palgrave Macmillan, Basingstoke and New York.

O'Brien, R.C., 2020. The Chinese Communist Party's ideology and global ambitions. The White House. www.whitehouse.gov/ briefings-statements/chinese-communist-partys-ideology-global-ambitions/ (accessed 21 October 2020).

O'Callaghan-Gordo, C. and Antó, J.M., 2020. COVID-19: The disease of the anthropocene. *Environmental Research* 187, 109683.

O'Harrow, R., 2020. Videos show closed-door sessions of leading conservative activists: 'Be not afraid of the accusations that you're a voter suppressor'. *Washington Post*.

Orbán, V., 2018. Prime Minister Viktor Orbán's speech at the final Fidesz election campaign event. Website of the Hungarian Government. www.kormany.hu/en/the-prime-minister/the-prime-minister-s-speeches/prime-minister-viktor-orban-s-speech-at-the-final-fidesz-election-campaign-event (accessed 20 April 2018).

Orbán, V., 2019. Prime Minister Viktor Orbán's speech at the 30th Bálványos Summer Open University and Student Camp. Website of the Hungarian Government. www.kormany.hu/en/the-prime-minister/the-prime-minister-s-speeches/prime-minister-viktor-orban-s-speech-at-the-30th-balvanyos-summer-open-university-and-student-camp (accessed 7 January 2020).

Oxfam International, 2020. *Time to Care: Unpaid and Underpaid Care Work and the Global Inequality Crisis.* Oxfam, Oxford.

Pandey, E., 2018. Caged giants: Why China's Big Tech can't escape the Communist Party. *Axios.* www.axios.com/china-big-tech-alibaba-tencent-communist-party-xi-jinping-c9de0516-1315-41e8-9daa-932c57f7faec.html (accessed 23 October 2020).

Parker, G., 2008. Crisis and catastrophe: The global crisis of the seventeenth century reconsidered. *The American Historical Review* 113, 1053–1079.

Partnership for Public Service, nd [rolling updates]. Political appointee tracker. Partnership for Public Service. https://ourpublicservice.org/political-appointee-tracker/ (accessed 28 October 2020).

Peck, J., 2001. Neoliberalizing states: Thin policies/hard outcomes. *Progress in Human Geography* 25, 445–455.

Pei, M., 2020. China's coming upheaval: Competition, the Coronavirus, and the weakness of Xi Jinping. *Foreign Affairs* 99, 82–95.

Pein, C., 2018. *Live Work Work Work Die: A Journey into the Savage Heart of Silicon Valley.* Scribe Publications, London.

Peischel, W., 2020. These five wildfire stats show just how devastating California's wildfires have been—so far. *Mother Jones.* www.motherjones.com/environment/2020/09/these-5-stats-show-just-how-devastating-californias-wildfires-have-been-so-far/ (accessed 2 November 2020).

Pettifor, A., 2006. *The Coming First World Debt Crisis*. Springer, Basingstoke and New York.

Pi, C., Rou, Z. and Horowitz, S., 2014. *Fair or Fowl? Industrialization of Poultry Production in China*. Institute for Agriculture and Trade Policy, Minneapolis.

Piketty, T., 2014. *Capital in the Twenty-First Century*. Harvard University Press, Cambridge, MA.

Plattner, M.F., 2019. Illiberal democracy and the struggle on the right. *Journal of Democracy* 30, 5–19.

Polanyi, K., 2001. *The Great Transformation: The Political and Economic Origins of Our Time*, 2nd edn. Beacon Press, Boston.

Popovich, N., Albeck-Ripka, L. and Pierre-Louis, K., 2020. The Trump administration is reversing nearly 100 environmental rules: Here's the full list. *New York Times* www.nytimes.com/interactive/2020/climate/trump-environment-rollbacks-list.html (accessed 21 March 2021).

Prochaska, F., 2012. John Stuart Mill: The tyranny of conformity, in *Eminent Victorians on American Democracy: The View from Albion*. Oxford University Press, Oxford, pp 23–46.

Pulido, L., Bruno, T., Faiver-Serna, C. and Galentine, C., 2019. Environmental deregulation, spectacular racism, and white nationalism in the Trump era. *Annals of the American Association of Geographers* 109, 520–532.

Qiang, X., 2019. The road to digital unfreedom: President Xi's surveillance state. *Journal of Democracy* 30, 53–67.

Raghunath, N., 2020. A sociological review of China's social credit systems and Guanxi opportunities for social mobility. *Sociology Compass* 14, e12783.

Randeria, S., 2019. Is each 'illiberal' democracy illiberal in its own way? LSE Brexit blog. https://blogs.lse.ac.uk/brexit/2019/11/28/are-all-liberal-democracies-alike-while-each-illiberal-democracy-is-illiberal-in-its-own-way/ (accessed 29 September 2020).

Raza, Z., 2019. China's 'political re-education' camps of Xinjiang's Uyghur Muslims. *Asian Affairs* 50, 488–501.

Renton, D., 2019. *The New Authoritarians: Convergence on the Right*. Pluto Press, London.

Renton, D., 2020. The new authoritarians: Revisiting the argument. *lives; running*, blog. https://livesrunning.wordpress.com/2020/05/02/the-new-authoritarian-revisiting-the-argument/ (accessed 12 May 2020).

Resnick, B., Fox, L., Volz, D. and Journal, N., 2015. Why four justices were against the Supreme Court's huge gay-marriage decision. *The Atlantic*. www.theatlantic.com/politics/archive/2015/06/why-four-justices-were-against-the-supreme-courts-huge-gay-marriage-decision/445932/ (accessed 27 October 2020).

Riesman, A., 2020. *12 Monkeys* is the apocalypse movie we need right now. *Vulture*. www.vulture.com/2020/03/12-monkeys-why-terry-gilliams-movie-is-so-relevant-today.html (accessed 13 August 2020).

Robertson, C., 2020. Coronavirus: Nine times Jair Bolsonaro dismissed the severity of COVID-19. *Sky News*. https://news.sky.com/story/coronavirus-nine-times-jair-bolsonaro-dismissed-the-severity-of-covid-19-12023297 (accessed 9 September 2020).

Rodríguez-Pose, A., 2018. The revenge of the places that don't matter (and what to do about it). *Cambridge Journal of Regions, Economy and Society* 11, 189–209.

Rogenhofer, J.M. and Panievsky, A., 2020. Antidemocratic populism in power: Comparing Erdoğan's Turkey with Modi's India and Netanyahu's Israel. *Democratization* 27:8, 1394–1412.

Root, D. and Barclay, A., 2018. Voter suppression during the 2018 midterm elections. Center for American Progress. www.americanprogress.org/issues/democracy/reports/2018/11/20/461296/voter-suppression-2018-midterm-elections/ (accessed 16 October 2020).

Rosenberg, J., 2003. *The Follies of Globalisation Theory: Polemical Essays*. Verso, London.

Rosenberg, J., 2006. Why is there no international historical sociology? *European Journal of International Relations* 12, 307–340.

Rosenberg, J. and Boyle, C., 2019. Understanding 2016: China, Brexit and Trump in the history of uneven and combined development. *Journal of Historical Sociology* 32, 32–58.

Ross, S., 2020. The 5 biggest Chinese software companies. *Investopedia*. www.investopedia.com/articles/markets/032616/5-biggest-chinese-software-companies-chl-tcehy.asp (accessed 23 October 2020).

Runciman, D., 2018. *How Democracy Ends*. Profile Books, London.

Rutland, P., 2014. The Pussy Riot affair: Gender and national identity in Putin's Russia. *Nationalities Papers* 42, 575–582.

Saez, E. and Zucman, G., 2019. *The Triumph of Injustice: How the Rich Dodge Taxes and How to Make Them Pay*. W.W. Norton & Company, New York.

Saull, R., 2014. The origins and persistence of the far right: Capital, class and the pathologies of liberal politics, in A. Anievas, N. Davidson, A. Fabry and R. Saull (eds), *Longue Durée of the Far-Right: An International Historical Sociology*. Routledge, Abingdon and New York, pp 21–43.

Scott, D., 2019. Bipartisan pushback against some environmental cuts. *Bloomberg Law*. https://news.bloomberglaw.com/environment-and-energy/bipartisan-pushback-against-some-environmental-cuts (accessed 28 October 2020).

Scott, R.E., 2020. We can reshore manufacturing jobs, but Trump hasn't done it: Trade rebalancing, infrastructure, and climate investments could create 17 million good jobs and rebuild the American economy. Economic Policy Institute. www.epi.org/publication/reshoring-manufacturing-jobs/ (accessed 21 October 2020).

Shaw, M., 2020. Political racism and the making of 'Brexitland'. *openDemocracy*. www.opendemocracy.net/en/can-europe-make-it/political-racism-and-the-making-of-brexitland/ (accessed 3 November 2020).

Sheerin, J., 2021. Biden: 'Police reaction would have been different if protesters were black'. *BBC News*. www.bbc.co.uk/news/live/election-us-2020-55558355/page/2 (accessed 2 February 2021).

Sherman, M. and Gresko, J., 2020. After RBG's death, 2 conservative justices take aim at 2015 decision legalizing same-sex marriage. *Time*. https://time.com/5896742/conservative-supreme-court-justices-target-gay-marriage/ (accessed 27 October 2020).

Shilliam, R., 2018. *Race and the Undeserving Poor (Building Progressive Alternatives): From Abolition to Brexit.* Agenda Publishing, Newcastle upon Tyne.

Shilliam, R., 2020. Enoch Powell: Britain's first neoliberal politician. *New Political Economy* 26:2 239–249.

Slobodian, Q., 2018. *Globalists: The End of Empire and the Birth of Neoliberalism.* Harvard University Press, Cambridge, MA and London.

Snyder, T., 2018. *The Road to Unfreedom: Russia, Europe, America,* iBook edn. Bodley Head, London.

Snyder, T., 2021. The American abyss. *New York Times.* www.nytimes.com/2021/01/09/magazine/trump-coup.html (accessed 21 March 2021).

Stiglitz, J., 2010. Contagion, liberalization, and the optimal structure of globalization. *Journal of Globalization and Development* 1, 1–47.

Stiglitz, J., 2019. *People, Power, and Profits: Progressive Capitalism for an Age of Discontent.* W.W. Norton & Company, New York.

Stonecash, J.M., 2017. The puzzle of class in presidential voting. *The Forum* 15, 29–49.

Sullivan, M., 2015. Ask the Vietnamese about war, and they think China, not the U.S. *National Public Radio.* www.npr.org/sections/parallels/2015/05/01/402572349/ask-the-vietnamese-about-war-and-they-think-china-not-the-u-s (accessed 8 September 2020).

Svolik, M.W., 2019. Polarization versus democracy. *Journal of Democracy* 30, 20–32.

Szabolcs, P., 2020. How Orbán played Germany, Europe's great power. *Direkt36.* www.direkt36.hu/en/a-magyar-nemet-kapcsolatok-rejtett-tortenete/ (accessed 5 October 2020).

Szöcsik, E. and Polyakova, A., 2019. Euroscepticism and the electoral success of the far right: The role of the strategic interaction between center and far right. *European Political Science* 18, 400–420.

Tatala, M., Rutynowska, E. and Wachowiec, P., 2020. *Rule of Law in Poland: A Diagnosis of the Deterioration of the Rule of Law from a Comparative Perspective.* Civil Development Forum, Warsaw.

Taylor, B.D., 2011. *State Building in Putin's Russia: Policing and Coercion after Communism*. Cambridge University Press, Cambridge.

Thatcher, M., 1987. Speech to Conservative Party Conference. Margaret Thatcher Foundation. www.margaretthatcher.org/document/106941 (accessed 13 October 2020).

The Information Office of the State Council, 2003. Full text of white paper on history and development of Xinjiang. http://en.people.cn/200305/26/eng20030526_117240.shtml (accessed 22 October 2020).

Thiel, P., 2009. The education of a libertarian. *Cato Unbound*. www.cato-unbound.org/2009/04/13/peter-thiel/education-libertarian (accessed 8 February 2021).

Thiel, P., 2016. Peter Thiel's entire Republican convention speech. www.youtube.com/watch?v=oUTnOQZOYv0 (accessed 21 March 2021).

Tocqueville, A., 2010. *Democracy in America*, 4 volume set. Liberty Fund, Indianapolis.

Tollefson, J., 2020. How hot will Earth get by 2100? *Nature* 580, 443–445.

Trotsky, L., 1904. Our political tasks. Marxist Internet Archive. www.marxists.org/archive/trotsky/1904/tasks/ (accessed 12 April 2013).

Trump, D., 2016. Read Donald Trump's speech on trade. *Time*. https://time.com/4386335/donald-trump-trade-speech-transcript/ (accessed 21 October 2020).

Trump, D., 2017. The inaugural address. The White House. www.whitehouse.gov/briefings-statements/the-inaugural-address/ (accessed 7 November 2020).

Trump, D., 2020a. This is the place where Pennsylvania workers made America into the most powerful nation in the world. Donald Trump YouTube Channel. www.youtube.com/watch?v=gKpWK2X6ZPs (accessed 21 March 2021).

Trump, D., 2020b. Homeless veteran gets 2nd chance. Donald Trump YouTube Channel. www.youtube.com/watch?v=Q6u9c8y_JgM (accessed 21 March 2021).

Trump, D., 2020c. President Donald Trump: White supremacist group Proud Boys should "stand back and stand by." www.youtube.com/watch?v=JZk6VzSLe4Y (accessed 21 March 2021).

Trump, D., 2020d. Twitter video of Trump return to the White House following hospitalisation. Twitter. https://twitter.com/realDonaldTrump/status/1313267143232942081 (accessed 19 October 2020).

Trump, D., 2020e. Donald Trump tweet comparing Coronavirus to flu. Twitter. https://twitter.com/realDonaldTrump/status/1313449844413992961 (accessed 19 October 2020).

Trump, D., 2020f. Donald Trump tweeting claiming immunity. Twitter. https://twitter.com/realDonaldTrump/status/1315316071243476997 (accessed 19 October 2020).

Trump, D., 2020g. Army for Trump. www.armyfortrump.com/ (accessed 19 October 2020).

Trump, D., 2020h. Donald Trump tweet calling for election day monitor. Twitter. https://twitter.com/realDonaldTrump/status/1316769383990153216 (accessed 19 October 20).

Trump, D., 2020i. Trump: 'I am your president of law and order'. *CBS News*. www.youtube.com/watch?v=1V46JPtj31s&t=317s (accessed 21 March 2021).

Trump, D., 2020j. Remarks by President Trump at the 2020 Council for National Policy Meeting. The White House. www.whitehouse.gov/briefings-statements/remarks-president-trump-2020-council-national-policy-meeting/ (accessed 26 October 2020).

UK Government, 2020. Coronavirus (COVID-19) in the UK: UK summary. *Coronavirus Data Gov.UK*. https://coronavirus.data.gov.uk/ (accessed 25 August 2020).

UNCTAD, 1997. *World Investment Report 1997: Transnational Corporations, Market Structure and Competition Policy*. United Nations, New York.

UNCTAD, 2019. *World Investment Report 2019: Special Economic Zones*. United Nations, New York.

UNHCR, 2019. UNHCR – global trends 2019: Forced displacement in 2019. UNHCR Global Trends 2019. www.unhcr.org/globaltrends2019/ (accessed 12 February 2021).

United Nations Development Programme, 2019. *Human Development Report 2019.* United Nations, New York.

United Nations General Assembly, 2007. *The United Nations Declaration on the Rights of Indigenous Peoples.*

Valluvan, S., 2019. *The Clamour of Nationalism: Race and Nation in Twenty-first-century Britain.* Manchester University Press, Manchester.

van der Pijl, K., 2012. *The Making of an Atlantic Ruling Class*, 2nd revised edn. Verso Books, London and Brooklyn.

Varshney, A., 2019. Modi consolidates power: Electoral vibrancy, mounting liberal deficits. *Journal of Democracy* 30, 63–77.

Vietnamese Government, 2020. Công suất xét nghiệm COVID-19 của Việt Nam được nâng lên rõ rệt – Chi tiết – Bộ Y tế – Trang tin về dịch bệnh viêm đường hô hấp cấp COVID-19. https://ncov.moh.gov.vn/web/guest/-/cong-suat-xet-nghiem-covid-19-cua-viet-nam-uoc-nang-len-ro-ret (accessed 25 August 2020).

Vu, K., Nguyen, P. and Pearson, J., 2020. After aggressive mass testing, Vietnam says it contains coronavirus outbreak. *Reuters.* www.reuters.com/article/us-health-coronavirus-vietnam-fight-insi-idUSKBN22B34H (accessed 21 March 2021).

Wallace, J.L. and Weiss, J.C., 2015. The political geography of nationalist protest in China: Cities and the 2012 anti-Japanese protests. *The China Quarterly* 222, 403–429.

Wallace, R., 2016. *Big Farms Make Big Flu: Dispatches on Influenza, Agribusiness, and the Nature of Science.* Monthly Review Press, New York.

Wallerstein, I., 1999. *End of the World as We Know It: Social Science for the Twenty-First Century.* University of Minnesota Press, Minneapolis and London.

Wang, M., 2020. More evidence of China's horrific abuses in Xinjiang. Human Rights Watch. www.hrw.org/news/2020/02/20/more-evidence-chinas-horrific-abuses-xinjiang (accessed 22 October 2020).

Wang, Z., 2013. The Chinese dream from Mao to Xi. *The Diplomat.* https://thediplomat.com/2013/09/the-chinese-dream-from-mao-to-xi/ (accessed 21 October 2020).

Watts, J., 2020. Alarm as Arctic sea ice not yet freezing at latest date on record. *The Guardian.* www.theguardian.com/world/2020/oct/22/alarm-as-arctic-sea-ice-not-yet-freezing-at-latest-date-on-record (accessed 21 March 2021) .

Watts, N., Amann, M., Arnell, N., Ayeb-Karlsson, S., Belesova, K., Boykoff, M., Byass, P., Cai, W., Campbell-Lendrum, D., Capstick, S., Chambers, J., Dalin, C., Daly, M., Dasandi, N., Davies, M., Drummond, P., Dubrow, R., Ebi, K.L., Eckelman, M., Ekins, P., Escobar, L.E., Montoya, L.F., Georgeson, L., Graham, H., Haggar, P., Hamilton, I., Hartinger, S., Hess, J., Kelman, I., Kiesewetter, G., Kjellstrom, T., Kniveton, D., Lemke, B., Liu, Y., Lott, M., Lowe, R., Sewe, M.O., Martinez-Urtaza, J., Maslin, M., McAllister, L., McGushin, A., Mikhaylov, S.J., Milner, J., Moradi-Lakeh, M., Morrissey, K., Murray, K., Munzert, S., Nilsson, M., Neville, T., Oreszczyn, T., Owfi, F., Pearman, O., Pencheon, D., Phung, D., Pye, S., Quinn, R., Rabbaniha, M., Robinson, E., Rocklöv, J., Semenza, J.C., Sherman, J., Shumake-Guillemot, J., Tabatabaei, M., Taylor, J., Trinanes, J., Wilkinson, P., Costello, A., Gong, P. and Montgomery, H., 2019. The 2019 report of The *Lancet* Countdown on health and climate change: Ensuring that the health of a child born today is not defined by a changing climate. *The Lancet* 394, 1836–1878.

Wellings, B., 2020. Brexit, nationalism and disintegration in the European Union and the United Kingdom. *Journal of Contemporary European Studies* iFirst, 1–13.

White, H., 1975. *Metahistory: The Historical Imagination in Nineteenth-century Europe.* Johns Hopkins University Press, Baltimore.

Wilczek, M., 2010. Smolensk: A decade since the air disaster that shook Poland. *Al Jazeera.* www.aljazeera.com/news/2020/04/smolensk-decade-air-disaster-shook-poland-200409230110957.html (accessed 5 August 2020).

Wodak, R., 2019. Entering the 'post-shame era': The rise of illiberal democracy, populism and neo-authoritarianism in Europe. *Global Discourse* 9, 195–213.

Wong, S., 2018. Video: Pro-Beijing protesters condemn HKU academic Benny Tai over independence remarks. *Hong Kong Free Press*. https://hongkongfp.com/2018/04/13/video-pro-beijing-protesters-condemn-hku-academic-benny-tai-independence-remarks/ (accessed 22 October 2020).

World Health Organization, 2020a. *Report of the WHO-China Joint Mission on Coronavirus Disease 2019 (Covid-19), 16–24 February 2020*. World Health Organization, Geneva.

World Health Organization, 2020b. Global Health Observatory: Medical doctors. https://apps.who.int/gho/data/node.main.HWFGRP_0020?lang=en (accessed 21 August 2020).

Xi, J., 2015. *The Governance of China*, iBook edn. BetterLink Press, Beijing.

Xiuzhong Xu, V., Cave, D., Leibold, J., Munro, K. and Ruser, N., 2020. *Uyghurs for Sale*. Australian Strategic Policy Institute, Canberra.

Yarvin, C., 2009. Climategate: History's message. *Unqualified Reservations by Mencius Moldbug*, blog. www.unqualified-reservations.org/2009/12/climategate-historys-message/ (accessed 8 February 2021).

Yarvin, C., 2019. The clear pill, part 1 of 5: The four-stroke regime. *The American Mind*. https://americanmind.org/salvo/the-clear-pill-part-1-of-5-the-four-stroke-regime/ (accessed 8 February 2021).

Zakaria, F., 1997. The rise of illiberal democracy essay. *Foreign Affairs* 76, 22–43.

Zeballos-Roig, J., 2020. 'Shameful!': AOC just delivered a 60-second takedown of Republicans who fought for a corporate bailout in the $2 trillion coronavirus aid bill. *Business Insider*. www.businessinsider.com/aoc-takedown-republicans-coronavirus-relief-bill-stimulus-corporate-bailouts-speech-2020-3 (accessed 23 October 2020).

Zhao, T. and Leibold, J., 2020. Ethnic governance under Xi Jinping: The centrality of the United Front Work Department and its implications. *Journal of Contemporary China* 29, 487–502.

Zuboff, S., 2019. *The Age of Surveillance Capitalism: The Fight for a Human Future at the New Frontier of Power*. Profile Books, London.

Index